# JOHN DEWEY

*This book is one of a series called
"Ethical Culture Publications"
published in collaboration with
the American Ethical Union.*

# JOHN DEWEY

THE RECONSTRUCTION OF THE
DEMOCRATIC LIFE

*Jerome Nathanson*

FREDERICK UNGAR PUBLISHING CO.
*NEW YORK*

*To*
ROSAM

# ACKNOWLEDGMENTS

D ESPITE the myth of objectivity, everyone's interpretation of another person is peculiarly his own. I am altogether mindful of this fact in the present interpretation of John Dewey. While this is "my" Dewey, I am hopeful that it will prove to be the Dewey of others as well—not simply because there is ample warrant in the texts for my interpretation, but because it seems to me so deeply relevant to the present condition of mankind.

My chief indebtedness in this work is to Dewey himself. His writings have been part of me since I first reached intellectual awareness. In subsequent years, my opportunities for face-to-face relations with him have been a privilege beyond acknowledgment.

As for the manuscript itself, I have special thanks for the criticisms and suggestions of Professor Justus Buchler of Columbia University and Professor Evelyn Urban Shirk of Hofstra College. If I have not always heeded them, I have nevertheless profited greatly from the comments of Professor Joseph L. Blau of Columbia University, Mr. Gideon Chagy, editor of *The Standard,* Mr. Lawrence K. Frank, Dr. Milton R. Sapirstein, and Dr. V. T. Thayer. The response of Mr. Charles Scribner, Jr., has meant a great deal to me. Many friends and acquaintances were kind enough to give me their appraisals of Dewey's influence in the fields of their specialization. Mrs. Beverly Gerber has been of help in many ways other than in the typing of the manuscript.

Only I can be fully aware of my immeasurable debt to Hiram Haydn, but I hope he has some sense of my feeling about it. And if it were not for my wife, I am sure I could not fulfill all of my regular professional obligations, to say nothing of writing books— her skill as an editor being just another bonanza.

# CONTENTS

JOHN DEWEY

# CHAPTER ONE

# PHILOSOPHY AND HUMAN PROBLEMS

THE year 1859 walked calmly across the pages of history, but it cast its shadow before it—a shadow whose length we still cannot accurately measure. It was a year of omens, if any had been shrewd enough to read them. No one was. It was also a year of great promises, far transcending the hopes of even the most sanguine of Victorians.

It was a tremendous year. It was then that Darwin published his *Origin of Species.* To be sure, he did not there "prove" the fact of evolution, but he made such a convincing case of the fact that human beings are part of nature that theologians and metaphysicians, to say nothing of naïve fundamentalists, have still not made their peace with his work. It was then that Marx published his *Critique of Political Economy,* and if it was later to be absorbed and half-forgotten in the light of *Das Kapital,* it nevertheless contained the powder of revolutions we may yet see explode. It was then that Bismarck was perfecting his plans for the Prussian chain reaction that was to immerse mankind in the greatest blood baths of all time. It was then that John Brown followed his chosen path from Harpers Ferry to the gallows, merging not only with the long lines of blue and gray, but with the forces of an industrial revolution that have changed the face of the earth.

How are we to measure the significance of historic events? Three days after John Brown tried to start an insurrection in Virginia, John Dewey was born in the back country of Vermont.

1

Whether the martyrdom of the one or the birth of the other was to have more important consequences for man, it is impossible to tell.

There is a simplicity and ruggedness about northern New England, especially Vermont, which can be oversentimentalized but not overstressed. The country is not lush nor easily fruitful, but a man willing to work can make a living, and one with "getup" can make his place. The hills roll away on every side, and if they lack the grandeur of the Rockies, they are humanly more manageable, easier to take inside oneself, giving a man less sense of his unimportance in the universe and more the feel of his own standing in the scheme of things. But above all, it is a place with roots, where the past is more than the weight of a weary tradition, for it comes alive in the ongoing present, and where unschooled men quote John Milton to their children.

The philosophy of John Dewey is the philosophy of democracy. This is not to say that he invented or created it. Obviously, he did neither. What he did was to give a creative, a growing edge to the life he inherited from the family line that started here in the 1630's and that was part of the air he breathed in Civil War and Reconstruction Vermont. His early schooling was here, a schooling that was more than a matter of schools and one that was to play an indispensable part not only in his philosophy of education, but in the formation of it. It was out of this early Vermont experience that democracy became part of the marrow of his bones.

From the public schools he went on to the University of Vermont, joining the brother who had preceded him, Davis R., who was to become one of America's most distinguished economists. There he was touched by one or two fine teachers whose inspiration pulled him more and more into the vortex of philosophic thought. Following his graduation from college, he moved to Pennsylvania to become a schoolteacher. The lines of his life were already drawn, and he was a philosopher at heart if not by vocation. This means not simply that he was reading philosophy, but that he was trying to write it as well.

Philosophy in our day is so much a specialized profession—or, at least, the teaching of it—that it must be realized it was not always so. Until after the Civil War, instead of its being an independent subject of investigation, the colleges regarded it as handmaiden to religion. The colleges were denominational in origin, and since the guiding principle of the curriculum was sectarian religion (a principle which some of our contemporaries have been trying desperately to revive), it was not uncommon for the president himself to give the course or courses in philosophy. When that was not the case, the subject was most often in the hands of the professor of religion—a man who could teach not only theology and psychology, but that "natural philosophy" as well which has since been broken down into the various natural sciences. Lest he sound even more gigantic in his abilities and herculean in his labors than he was, we must remind ourselves that the accumulated knowledge in these fields, as compared with today, was in the ratio of an abridged dictionary, pocket size, to an encyclopedia. Even more important, the concern was not with laboratory techniques and the learning of methods of investigation but with "learning" what was already "known."

More than a generation earlier, Emerson had issued our declaration of cultural independence in his classic address on *The American Scholar*. We tend today to regard his message as commonplace enough, although we still have not taken seriously one of the chief things he was talking about. On the one side, Emerson was urging Americans to look on their own, unique experience with their own, distinctive eyes, expressing it in their individual ways instead of aping the attitudes and expressions of Europe. This lesson we learned, and Whitman was one of the first fruits of it. On the other side he was also pleading with us to become whole men, "man thinking," as he called it, instead of narrow specialists who could not see the relation of their work to the life of the community, to say nothing of the life of mankind.

A hundred years later, in the maturest of John Dewey's work, American culture had come full circle. We were more sophisticated, life was both more complicated and complex, and neither the conditions nor the problems at the dawn of the industrial age were the same as those facing us in its midday sun. No doubt because of these very differences, the problem on which Emerson fixed with prophetic insight was to become fraught with an increasing ominousness. And Dewey was to warn us again, in countless pages of his writings, that the only hope for us lay in seeing ourselves as part of a larger whole, in seeing the creative relation between the individual and the community.

Meanwhile, we achieved independence with such a vengeance that we did not know how to use our power. As a nation, we vacillated between isolating ourselves in our newly created might and using that might isolatedly to force others to do our will. Within the nation, the businessman dominated more and more of our life in the spirit of a narrow commercialism, asking only that he be let alone. The scientist retreated more and more into the ivory tower of his laboratory, asking only, until he produced the atom bomb, that he be let alone. And the philosopher, poor fellow, laboring over abstruse and sometimes irrelevant questions, was generally ignored.

But a great deal had happened before that point was reached. The Civil War had unleashed such tremendous forces that the face of American civilization was transformed. It was not simply that the railroad had reached across the continent, eventually to make of the westward trek of the pioneers one of the great migrations of human history. It was not simply the piling up of people in dirty and depersonalized cities, a process the sociology books euphemistically call the urbanizing of civilization. It was not simply the denuding of the forest lands, which was to end in converting fertile soil into dust bowls and deserts. All that was serious enough. But much graver in its repercussions on human beings and their relations to each other was the way it divorced a man's work from his living, and sank him in the drudgery of routinized if remunerative labor.

It is this vast problem which shadows us all; but we have not begun to see it clearly, let alone to solve it. And it is this problem which is the backdrop of the incredible specialization of modern life, where physicians are subdivided into experts on internal medicine and surgery, surgeons further subdivided into experts on the ear and the appendix, and so on. One of the serious consequences is that while only a rare physician understands what a higher mathematician is doing, the expert on the appendix does not even understand the finer points of aural surgery. Needless to say, the same thing holds true of every specialization in our society, including all those not dignified by the name of "profession." It is in the light of these developments that we have to view the specialization of science and philosophy.

As one result of this process, philosophy was separated from religion, with the colleges establishing separate departments for each subject. It was essentially part of the broader process we have mentioned. Men are not puppets jiggled by historical forces, however, nor even merely the agents of those forces. Human beings collectively, and the nature to which they belong, *are* the forces, and it is mystic mumbo jumbo to believe otherwise. In this separation of philosophy and religion, individuals played a creative part. In America, one man more than any other contributed to wresting philosophy from the control of the clergy. That was W. T. Harris, later U. S. Commissioner of Education, who in his earlier years worked indefatigably to bring Hegelian philosophy to Americans and to make philosophers of some of them. One result of his efforts and of those of others was that the teaching of philosophy gradually gained recognition as a self-respecting profession on its own.

All this was of critical importance in the life of Dewey. Had he been born fifty years sooner, whatever else he might have become, it is not likely he would have been the professional philosopher we know; or, if he had, he would have faced quite a different job from the one that confronted him. As matters stood, with Harris furthering the philosophic enterprise from his headquarters in St. Louis, it seemed that philosophy might offer a career to an able young man. It might, but could it? How was one to get, if not a guarantee, at least a reasonably practical answer to the question? Harris himself might supply it. After some concentrated reading in philosophy, therefore, Dewey sent some of his writing to the mentor of the movement. Harris encouraged him, and a career was decided. Shortly afterward, the young Vermonter traveled to Baltimore and began his studies in the graduate school of Johns Hopkins University.

Those were the days when there was in the graduate schools of America an intellectual ferment that brewed greatness. A generation earlier, the country had many colleges but no genuine universities. A generation later, the universities were becoming the Ph.D. belt lines that have made them as efficient and impersonalized as big business. But in the seventies and eighties the ferment was bubbling, and professors and students were joined in the enthusiasm of creation. In their approach to scholarship, to be sure, they bore the mark fathered on them by the German universities, a mark that in many of the offspring became the hereditary brand of pedantry. Yet they were lifted up by a common spirit and fired by a sense of their mission. Gilman at Johns Hopkins, Eliot at Harvard, White at Cornell, these and a handful of others were the master builders, building universities into the central structure of American life; and though we sometimes distrust "intellectuals" and fear "brain-trusts," in moments of perspective we know that our society could not function if it were not fed by the universities which these men and their followers created.

This was the creative atmosphere in which Dewey lived at Hopkins. When he finished his work there, he was a scholar—enough of a scholar, indeed, not to have to display the apparatus of his scholarship. Only one already possessed of a fair knowledge of the history of thought can appreciate the time and labor that lie behind his profound insights and discussions of this thinker or that movement.

Now as part of the intellectual climate covering the continent, the spirit of German scholarship in the universities had as its counterpart the propagandizing and dominance of German philosophy, a condition that antedated the rise of the universities themselves. Long before, the poet Coleridge had galvanized the

cultured circles of the English-speaking world with his revela-
tions from German philosophy. Edward Everett and some of his
colleagues at Harvard gave them a base in this country. Emerson
reveled in them, arrowing the message to enchanted audiences
throughout the Chautauqua circuit. And lesser workers in the
vineyard made the soil more favorable to their domestic growth.
It was no wonder, then, that young men dedicated to pursuing
the life of the mind went to Germany to study. Germany was
scholarship and *Gemütlichkeit,* Germany was beauty and learning, Germany was truth and romance—in a word, Germany was
culture.

It was almost impossible for an earnest, intellectual young
man not to be mastered by this influence, and though a few
escaped its domination, Dewey was not one of them. He was,
when he finished Hopkins, as much under the thumb of the great
German thinkers as any of his contemporaries. More specifically,
due to his teacher and later colleague, George Sylvester Morris,
and due partly to the influence of the Harris circle, he was under
Hegel's hypnotic spell.

Hegel was a sprawling thinker, and it is sometimes impossible to know what he meant. However sacrilegious it may sound,
it is probable that this was because sometimes he himself did not
know what he meant—a common human failing, to which philosophers are as susceptible as any others and for which, by the
same token, they are no more blameworthy. In Hegel's case, the
waters are further muddied by his complicated style of writing.
Bad writing, as distinguished from difficult thinking, is by no
means a philosophic necessity, as the works of Plato and Aristotle
plainly show. In the entire history of philosophy, indeed, it is seldom a quality of the great thinkers, until we reach Kant and some
of his successors in 19th century Germany. Then it seemed for a
certain period to become a virtue, with the presumption that
simple writing is superficial, while anything we have to sweat to
understand must be deep. This "logic" reached its greatest absurdity in the experience with one of Kant's own important works:
some pages of it were inadvertently put in the wrong place by the

printer (pages beginning, not with a new section, but in the middle of a thought), and the error was not discovered for a century! In the intervening years, learned men wrote learned comments on this abstruse passage. This is only a glaring instance of many others which might be cited to show the common obeisance to "profundity." However that may be, if complicated writing is a virtue, Hegel must surely be ranked as the most virtuous of philosophers.

Despite this, or perhaps in a measure because of it, he is undoubtedly one of the most influential thinkers in history. Philosophers who followed loved or hated him, but for two generations at least they did not often ignore him. Further, scholars in other fields were infected by the virus, and although they may be unaware of it, many Americans walking the streets at the present time studied English literature in school and college in the spirit of Hegel. Nor could communism in the modern world have been what it is were it not for him, for he was half the inspiration and a good part of the intellectual method of Karl Marx.

Why, in his first philosophic period, Dewey was so deeply drawn to Hegel it is hard to say. The dominance of German thought in American universities and in the thinking of some of the teachers who influenced him most is not sufficient to account for it, since some of his contemporaries, educated under the same general influence, found the path leading back to Kant and had no use for Hegel. It might be said in explanation that it was a question of temperament, which James regarded as the base of all philosophic leanings—but this seems to be a poor hypothesis in view of the fact that persons of similar temperaments often hold sharply different philosophies, and the other way around. The probability is, rather, that it comes down to two basic ideas or attitudes: the ideas of evolution and organic growth, the attitudes of history and biology. Both these are so deep in the mind of Dewey that they remained central to his thinking after he abandoned Hegel. In the early years, it seems reasonable to assume, he was captivated by Hegel's thought because it offered what appeared to be a suitable philosophic framework for these approaches to life.

Today, the theory of evolution is part of the mental landscape of all educated persons. In the light of current tempers of mind, the famous Scopes trial in Tennessee seems to have taken place not merely a generation ago but in a much more distant past. No doubt our faith in "progress" has been shaken if not destroyed by the events of the last two decades. Even faith in moral evolution, and in the perfectibility of man, has taken a merciless pounding from our recent experiences of human bestiality. The idea that man has risen from less-developed forms of animal being, however, and that all forms of many-celled life are rooted in simpler forms that preceded them—this idea of evolution is now part of the mentality of all but certain religious fundamentalists.

It was quite a different situation when Dewey was studying at Hopkins and in the period immediately following when he was teaching philosophy at the universities of Michigan and Minnesota. That was the heyday of the controversy between the traditional belief, that man and every other species had been created as they now were, and the new vision. In England and America alike, Darwinism became a gospel to be preached with missionary zeal, or to be fought as a major heresy by defenders of the old faith. The battle lines had been drawn earlier, the opposing sides marshaling their forces in this country while the nation was fighting the Civil War. But it was in this later period that the major engagements were fought and the issue settled, even though it took another fifty years to make this clear.

To be sure, people were misled about the major issue, thinking of it as a struggle between science and theology—and many of us continue to think of it as just that. Darwin himself knew better, as Dewey has pointed out. For the real impact of the evolution theory, the impact of incalculable influence, was to be not on theology but on science and philosophy. This is so far from being apparent that many people, including scientists and philosophers, still do not see it. And, as we shall find later, Dewey's intellectual labors for half a century have been concentrated on this question to such an extent that his philosophy can be understood only in the light of it. This is the philosophy the world has come to know, a philosophy in which Hegel is of only indirect importance, and which received a tremendous push with the publication of William James's *Principles of Psychology* in 1890.

Prior to that date Dewey, together with others who were receptive to the theory of evolution, was faced with a special problem. Assuming that life is an evolving process, how did man get his "mind"? Evolution might give us the clue to how our bodies developed, but it seemed self-evident that the body was one thing and the mind quite another. While the bodies of less-developed forms of life might be conceived of as the springboard for the development of the human body, none of them has what we can honestly call "mind," let alone "soul." If our minds did evolve, then, from what did they evolve? Darwin might account for the origin of species, but he did not account for this. Who could, and how? Here was Hegel's importance for Dewey.

For Hegel was an "evolutionary" thinker. This is not to say that he was a Darwinian or anticipated Darwin. He was not and did not. Neither was he, to speak accurately, a scientific thinker. His whole sense of life was poles apart from the painstaking, investigating, experimental attitude of the scientist. His was a prescientific approach to evolution or development; and although the idea that species evolved from lower forms was compatible with what he thought and taught, it would not have occurred to him to think this way, let alone to carry on the observations and inquiries that would support the thesis.

What was usable in his philosophy for Dewey's purposes, however, was the notion that life is a process of growth and development. This idea had a philosophic past dating back to Aristotle. But it had never had the inclusiveness that Hegel gave it. For Aristotle, as for all thinkers until the nineteenth century, species were fixed, and one species could no more be the parent of another than an ant could father a sparrow. Such development as there was in life was always within a species, as in the growth of an oak from an acorn—and the limits of that growth were always somehow specified or preordained, in the sense that if an acorn completely fulfilled itself, it could never be anything but an oak. There was nothing so limited as this in Hegel's idea of things. For him, all things were part of a dynamic whole, the Absolute Idea (or God), which was not only responsible for everything that is, but was expressing or realizing itself in everything that is. All forms of being, animate and inanimate, vegetable and animal, inhuman and human, were manifestations of it. The Absolute expressed itself in matter and mind, in things and ideals, in individuals and societies. Because it was Idea as well as Absolute, it followed that its higher expressions were in mind rather than matter, in ideas and ideals rather than things. Because it was collective, gathering everything up into itself, it followed that its higher expressions were in societies rather than individuals—all individuals, that is, with the exception of Hegel himself. For he regarded the twin appearances of the Prussian state and of himself as its philosopher as the most complete manifestations of the Absolute up to that time.

The latter was an idea that never impressed Dewey favorably. On the contrary, at the beginning of World War I, this grandiose if not paranoid conception, which was a member of a whole German family of similar ideas, was responsible for one of Dewey's most biting polemics, *German Philosophy and Politics*. Hegel's fruitfulness for Dewey lay in the fact that he accounted for the appearance of "mind" in the process of evolution. In other words, he could supplement Darwin at just the point where help was most needed. As long as bodies and minds were regarded as separate entities, Darwin and Hegel seemed to be a good combination. Some of his writing in this period shows that Dewey was freeing himself from Hegel, but James completely liberated him and won his support in revolutionizing our conception of "mind."

Evolution, concerned with the development of all forms of life, is of course a broader category than human history. But history is the proper designation for what has happened to human beings. While both Hegel and Dewey are therefore broadly evolutionary thinkers in their approach to human affairs, their attitude is historical. How did a given state of things come to be? What is the relation of ideas to the culture in which they arise and play their part? What light does the history of an idea shed on its meaning? And if it does shed light, does that have any bearing on its validity or truth?

Questions of this kind, raised so spontaneously in our time, would not have seemed very weighty or important to most thinkers before the nineteenth century. They would not even have asked them. And if they had, they would not have meant the same things by them as we do. We walk the same earth, but we live in a different universe.

For example, we may marvel at the thought that in Greece, more than two thousand years ago, the philosopher Democritus said that all matter consists of atoms, thinking that he thus miraculously "anticipated" modern science. As a matter of fact, however, Democritus' solid little pellets have no more in common with the spacious particles of present-day physics than the mythical Icarus' wings have with a jet-propelled plane. Set down in the lecture room of a nuclear physicist, the ancient Greek would not know what the lecture was all about. Or, to take another example, it appears that everywhere and at all times people have wanted to account for the heartaches and evils of life. The story of Adam and Eve, and their eating of the forbidden fruit, "accounts" for it in one way. The story of Pandora's box "accounts" for it in another. But neither these nor hosts of stories like them have anything in common with the account of a cultural anthropologist.

The great scholar J. B. Bury has shown how recent in origin is the idea of progress. The same thing holds for the attitude of history as we understand it. And it holds especially for the historical attitude as brought to bear on ideas and truth. From the time Aristotle first formalized logic until only yesterday, as history goes, truth was thought to be timeless and unchanging. Men might be ignorant of a truth or, even worse, be guilty of error.

But once they discovered it, it was assumed that that truth had always been there to be discovered, and that it had always been just what it was. The idea that there might be an unfolding truth, manifesting itself in time and in different ways at different times, was as foreign as the idea of a growing and changing universe. How, then, could there be a history of truth? The notion was preposterous. All there could be was a history of the discovery of truth.

Yet Hegel not only entertained this preposterous notion, he built an entire philosophy around it. It must be admitted that he straddled the issue, attempting to have his cake and to eat it, too. That is, his Absolute Idea was Truth, and it would always be what it was, time without end. In this respect, he was as traditional as it is possible to be. But this was to look at things from an over-all point of view, cosmically. This is what the Absolute Idea would look like to a being outside it, which by definition, paradoxically, there could not be. Inside the cosmos or, more accurately, within the Absolute (which is where everything is), there was all the change and development that anyone could want or discover—and that held for truth as much as for anything else. Indeed, the only clue one could get to the essential nature of the Absolute was to discover the method by which truth developed in the course of time. This, according to Hegel, was just what he had discovered, the method of historical dialectic. The Absolute expressed itself in a given situation (the thesis); this situation produced its opposite number or contradiction (the antithesis); and a resolution of the conflict between the two was found in a new situation (the synthesis). The situations never repeat themselves, but the process has gone on from the beginning of time and will continue until the end of time.

It was this method, of course, that was so essential to Marx's thinking. He contended that Hegel had been standing on his head, and that he had put him rightside up—by which he meant that not an Idea but matter was basic to the universe, and that only from this starting point could the historical dialectic be properly understood. Thus Marx developed that materialist dialectic which is the essence of the communist philosophy, and whose practical edge in our time is the proposition that the capitalist class (the thesis) brought forth its opposite number, the working class (the antithesis), and that the conflict between the two will sometime find its resolution in a classless society (the synthesis). In other words, granted the change in starting point from Idea to matter, Hegel's dialectic method was exactly what was most important to Marx.

Such was not the case with Dewey, who seems to have been lured not at all by this neat, schematic sense of human development. It was the historical approach to ideas and to truth that was congenial to him. And though, as we shall see, he applied it differently and in doing so transformed its meaning, he was in the early years as sympathetically disposed to what Hegel attempted to do in this area as he was indebted to him in the field of evolution.

The whole question goes deeper and brings us face to face with one of the moot problems of contemporary thought. What we call the evolutionary approach or the historical attitude is technically labeled the genetic method. By and large, it assumes that we can get a better understanding of persons and situations if we look at them as processes, seeking their origins and tracing their development for what light they can throw on whatever is being examined or analyzed. In large measure, this is the method of psychoanalysis, which uses dreams, the free association of ideas and memories, and identification with the doctor in order to bring to consciousness important incidents in an adult's forgotten childhood—the assumption being that if we can only see clearly the origin of personality conflicts we can put them in a realistic setting and allay neurotic anxieties. The success of the genetic method in this and other fields is evidence that it can yield fruitful results. On the other hand, there is always the danger of committing what is called the genetic fallacy—that is, of assuming that an idea has or has not validity in the light of its history. As evidence of the truth or falsity of an idea the genetic method is demonstrably unreliable. By way of illustration, if it could be shown that Hitler was mentally unbalanced, that would not prove anything about any one of his ideas: the truth or falsity of the "master-race" fantasy would have to be established on other grounds.

In Dewey's work, the genetic method is frequently employed as a weapon in argument. It is a polemical device, through the use of which he undercuts another position by giving its history, as when he equates the separation of theory and practice in Greek thought with the existence of an aristocratic leisure class and an enslaved working class. The conclusion to be drawn is that no genuine democrat could possibly separate theory and practice. This may be true, but it does not follow from the argument, as nobody knows better than Dewey himself. For him, the path to truth lies not in any backward reference but in the experimental procedures of science. In all such arguments, therefore, it is as if he were saying that the "exposing" of an idea is sometimes more effective than its careful examination. And it is. Yet the affair is not quite so simple as this. For beyond the question of polemical effectiveness, the historical attitude or genetic method has a great deal to do with what Dewey means by philosophy. This is an issue to which we shall have to return.

In addition to the evolutionary idea or historical attitude, Dewey was drawn to Hegel because of the latter's stress on organic growth and unity. One of the dominant traditions of Western thought has been the separating of things into appearance and reality. Plato, whose philosophy can be interpreted in different ways, is thought by many to have given this notion its classic formulation, though even thus interpreted the split between the two domains was not as sharp as it later became.

The world of experience, the world in which we carry on our day-to-day existence, according to this understanding of Plato, is not what the world "really" is. What we experience is a business of comings and goings, growth and decadence, birth and death— in a word, we experience constant flux or change. But whatever is real must be lasting and perfect: lasting because, by definition, reality is what endures; perfect because only what is perfect has no need to change into something else. Behind experience, or the appearances of things, therefore, is Reality. A human being changes from infancy through childhood through maturity to senility, and yet remains the "same" person. How can this be? The dualistic tradition would answer that behind all the apparent changes is the "real" person, the "soul" of Christian theology. So in all things. There are many goods in life, but behind them all is the "real," exemplary, highest Good.

This belief has many important consequences. We can have opinions about the world of experience, but genuine knowledge only about Reality. We can experience things emotionally, but know them only through Reason. A farmer can till the soil and a doctor practice medicine, but such practices can at best yield only faint glimmerings of a sound theory of things. A person can live among temporal changes, but he can find his real being, the meaning of life, only by contemplation of what is unchanging and eternal. These dualisms—between appearance and reality, opinion and knowledge, emotion and reason, practice and theory, temporal and eternal—have trapped the mind of Western man for twenty-five hundred years, and countless persons, including some of the most gifted, have agonized over the problems that stemmed from them.

For Plato himself, however interpreted, the separation between the two worlds was never complete. Men might live in a world of shadows, but they were at least shadows of Reality, and there was a path, however dimly marked, from one to the other. Men might live in the world and yet transcend it. Indeed, they could do more. They could remake it in the light of what they perceived of ultimate Truth.

In the extreme reaches of Christian theology, however, the split between the two worlds was total. Only the soul could have possible contact with the Reality which was God, and that contact could be established, not through any method known to man, but only through the miraculous intervention of God's grace. It is no wonder, then, that many of the best Christian spirits, believing the world of experience to be both a delusion and a snare, chose to give up "the world." For them, the monastic life or the hermit's solitude, if it could not guarantee grace, was at least a defense against being beguiled by "appearance." What modern psychiatry might label escapism or retreat from reality, therefore, was on their theory of life just the reverse. And history has seen no greater irony than this: that the ethics of Jesus, which were devised to help men better to make their way in the world, should have led to a philosophy and religion that moved them to withdraw from it.

But philosophers and theologians are not the only ones who have first predicated and then struggled with these dualisms. There have been scientists, too, who were kindred spirits. Such are those chemists who separate water into hydrogen and oxygen and then solemnly assure us that no matter what water appears to be, this is what it "really" is. Such are those physicists who assure us that the floors we walk on or the chairs we sit in are "really" nothing but billions of electrons flying through space. These, and numbers of others like them, have used the language of modern science to perpetuate the age-long split between appearance and reality.

Now Hegel, as had Spinoza before him, completely undercut this dualism. For him, however and wherever else the Absolute Idea might be working itself out, it was certainly manifesting itself in the world of experience. To set appearance off against reality was, in Hegel's terms, the sheerest nonsense, literally non-sense. Experience was Reality and Reality was experience. Whatever is, by definition, is real. And the problem of philosophy is not the boondoggling venture of finding out what relation experience has to reality. The problem is to find out what relations actually exist in experience. According to Hegel, things do not exist in themselves and have relations to other things. On the contrary, they exist *in* their relations. Things are interrelated, interdependent. And they have a unity that comes about by virtue of their being expressions of the Absolute. It is this interrelated unity in an evolving universe that is the meaning of organic growth. Again, as is true of the other phases of his indebtedness to Hegel, Dewey has given this conception a different context and a different meaning. But it is significant that, half a century after he had apparently parted company with Hegel, he could still refer to experience as "a moving whole of interacting parts."

From one point of view, this organic idea need have nothing to do with the biologic attitude. Such diverse philosophers of history as Spengler and Toynbee have had an organic sense of cultures—speaking of their birth, maturity, senescence, and death, in exact analogy to individual organisms—while having no real sympathy with attempts to account for such developments "naturally." That is, they have appealed to something beyond nature —to God, or Fate, or the Unknowable, or Force—to "explain" what has happened. Toynbee, for example, assumes that the Christian epic is the obvious meaning of history, although to one nurtured on the Upanishads it might not be obvious at all but merely wishful thinking on Toynbee's part. For all such thinkers, the organic movement of things is comprehensible only by appealing to something that transcends it. In other words, their attitude is the reverse of the biologist's (when he is functioning as a biologist, it is important to remember, and not as a metaphysician or theologian). For the biologist is concerned not with transcending nature but with showing the developmental relations of life within nature.

As we have seen, the Absolute Idea played a dual role for Hegel. But the effort to discover the relationships through which it expressed itself kept him within nature. That is another reason why the substance of what he was saying, as distinguished from his dialectic method, had such an impact on Dewey. Hegel was a weapon for fighting the dualisms of the influential neo-Kantian philosophers. He was a means of giving to philosophy the continuity that Dewey found in experience.

Yet looking back, we can see that Hegel's philosophic effort was part of the sunset glow of an age that was passing away. He gathered together, with a certain magnificence, the ranks of that eighteenth-century civilization that had been shattered by the great revolutions. Child of the Enlightenment, as were Wordsworth and Beethoven, he tried to give rational order to the universe of thought as they tried to give it to literature and music. But his system was imposed upon the flux of life, and it could no more withstand the onrushing developments of a new age than Napoleon's continental system could unify Europe.

For the new age was bound to burst the seams of every philosophic system, exactly as it smashed the old confines of civilization itself. Industrialism and technology, locomotives and dynamos, mass production and gigantic corporations—these were not simply names on the pages of books and magazines. They were the new facts of life or, if you will, the facts of a new life. They arose in response to problems created by human needs, in turn to create their own problems, then leading men to invent the methods of dealing with them. We are still so caught up in this vast interlacing of events that most of the time we cannot see it, let alone understand what it means or where it is moving. If we want a name for it, we can say it is the greatest revolution since human beings invented language and learned to use their hands for making tools. For its impact will prove to be, even more than on the things with which we live, on the ways we see things and each other, and on the ways we live.

It was in this world, in which the lid was blasted off, that the Dewey who started as a Hegelian slowly fashioned his own revolutionary philosophy. He did so in an atmosphere of widespread intellectual eruption. Mathematics and physics, seemingly so settled, suddenly pushed across the boundaries and became, in effect, new sciences. Chemistry, biology, physiology, psychology, anthropology, sociology, all these and other disciplines, as we know them, were born in Dewey's own lifetime. Frederick Jackson Turner, Charles A. Beard, James Harvey Robinson, and their followers, contemporaries and colleagues of Dewey's, blazed new trails in their study of history. Henry George and Thorstein Veblen gave an institutional dimension to economics. There is not a phase of mental activity, as eventually there will not be a phase of human culture, not transformed by the new vision. Civilization erupted volcanically, and the lava covered the earth.

What, in such a world, is the role of the philosopher? What, indeed, is philosophy? To answer these questions has been the burden of Dewey's work. And one of the major clues to his handling of them was the psychology of James. For James's *Psychology* was a landmark in the history of man's intellectual life. His conception of the "stream of thought" has been notably influential, in literature perhaps even more than in psychology and psychiatry. But for Dewey and others, this idea was of minor import compared with James's biological approach to human behavior, his careful investigations into the ways in which the human organism adjusts itself to its environment and adapts the environment to its needs.

Previously, psychology had assumed the existence of the "soul" to account for all such matters. James, without deciding the metaphysical question of the soul's existence, attempted to construct a psychology that was independent of the assumption. Just as astronomy, physics, and chemistry had developed as sciences when they turned their backs on metaphysical speculation, so James proposed that a science of human behavior depended upon the same attitude. Accordingly, he examined the physiological mechanisms that make possible our "mental" activity, and as adequately as he could he proceeded on this basis to account for the habits that play so overwhelming a part in human experience, developing as well new theories of memory, of interest and attention, and of the emotions.

As is true with Darwin in the field of evolution, James's tremendous significance for psychology lay less in what he accomplished than in his attempt, in the spirit and direction of his efforts. And while steadfastly refusing to tie psychology to any species of supernaturalism (actually, in his own life, instead of being neutral he was a forthright theist), he revolutionized our thinking about man. After all, theology, by and large, rested on the proposition that every person had a God-given soul, which was not only the key to possible salvation but the essence of the *human* being. If, now, human behavior could be explained without relying on the notion of the soul, what would happen to man's relations to the churches, to say nothing of other institutions? What would happen to the churches themselves, and to their sense of the meaning of the human enterprise? No one can give the answers to these questions, for we are in the midst of working them out. But it is clear that James, whatever his own desires, contributed as much as any other one person to the rise of the new humanism.

In his later philosophic work, he went even further, and here it seems that Dewey influenced him as much as he did Dewey. What the "soul" had been to psychology, the "mind" or "consciousness" had been to philosophy. We think because we have minds, it seemed obvious to everyone. How, then, are our minds related to our bodies, on the one side, and to the world in which we live, on the other? How can we know anything? If mind and matter are radically different stuff, every phase of their relation is a problem, if not a mystery. But what if there is no such entity as "mind" or "consciousness"? What if, instead of thinking and talking about bodies *having* minds, we think of organisms that function physically and mentally? This is precisely what James did. He assumed that "consciousness" does not exist. This does not mean the absurdity of thinking that human beings are not conscious. It does mean that behaving consciously is a biologic function exactly as are eating and breathing.

All this gave Dewey a wide-open universe in which to carry on his philosophic work. If human behavior could be accounted for biologically, if "mind" and "body" were not separate entities, then neither Hegel's nor any corresponding species of idealism was intellectually necessary. The evolution of the human organism would be accounted for without appealing to anything beyond nature. The dualisms between appearance and reality, mind and body, knowledge and opinion, facts and ideals, could be undercut without relying on an Absolute Idea. Ideas and knowledge could be seen as instruments developed by the living organism for making its way in the world of which it was part. Through the new psychology of habit, the dynamic relations of individual and society could be better seen, for individual habits are shaped by our social institutions—by the family, language, schools; by the ways in which we conduct our economic, political, and social affairs; by recreation and by religion—by all the things that are as much part of each of us as the air we breathe or the food we eat.

It was in terms of these new insights that philosophy became, for Dewey, an undertaking radically different from anything he, or most other thinkers, had previously thought it to be. Traditionally, the aim of most philosophers was to develop a system that would give the most inclusive and truest account of the universe. Different phases of their thinking were taken as either true or false, and in so far as they were true, they would be true for all time. From this point of view, it would be ridiculous to say, as Dewey has said, that the degree to which Aristotle's logic was adapted to the conditions of ancient Greece, to just that degree it is not adapted to the needs of the modern world.

But shift the viewpoint from philosophy as a system-building enterprise, and something basic happens. Philosophy can then be seen as part of man's effort to make his way in the world. Man has ambitions, ideals, dreams, perspectives. These do not come out of the air, but out of the conditions of life. Thinking is an attempt to solve problems, to solve them in ways that will help us to attain whatever goals we have in mind. The problems themselves arise out of the institutions and relations of our common life, and the goals, too, have their origins there. The process of history is a process of change—changes of institutions, of habits, of problems, of expectations, of ideals. What philosophy does is give us a sense of direction through the complexities of life. It does not solve problems of day-to-day existence, for they can be solved only in the situations in which they arise, but it can help us to see how the problems might be solved. It does not create the values or ideals by which we live, but it can help us to clarify them, to evaluate them, to see them in perspective. From this point of view it is obvious—is it not—that in so far as Aristotle performed this function for the world in which he lived, he cannot do it for ours.

Meaning is broader than truth, as we shall see in what follows, and the meaning of life is man's primary concern. To say that a philosopher is not the architect of a system of truth, accordingly, is not to belittle him. It is, on the contrary, to offer him a greater dignity. For philosophy, as everything else, arises out of the problems of men. And the philosopher can help us all immeasurably as he contributes whatever he can to making human life more meaningful.

# CHAPTER TWO

# THE WORLD WE LIVE IN

N O ONE but a philosopher could ever doubt that the world exists. For the rest of us, the joys and sorrows, the successes and failures, the goods and evils of existence are just what they appear to be: the real experiences of real people in a real world. We have problems because the world is once and for all the kind of world in which problems arise, just as it is the kind of world in which fish swim and birds fly. In our more speculative moments, we may ask ourselves *why* there is a world, and some people assume that this is a meaningful question to which meaningful answers can be given. But once grant that there is a world, and it seems peculiarly pointless to ask why it is the kind of world it happens to be. It is what it is, and most of us never needed Carlyle to tell us we had better accept it.

To be completely candid, of course, not even philosophers have doubted the world's existence. They have, in their individual ways, lived their day-to-day lives just as do the rest of us. For them, too, bread and wine, sunsets and symphonies, friendship and love have been of genuine significance. Offhand, one would surmise that such experiences would have a good deal to do with their philosophies. All too frequently, they have not, and this is one reason why some philosophers seem to have nothing whatever to do with the problems of men.

This is not to say that philosophers are whimsical or arbitrary or simply foolish. Some of them are all these things, and all of them are, sometime or other, one of them. On the whole, however, they are a remarkably intelligent class of human beings, and the wisest of them have been among the great ones of the earth. How does it happen, then, that some of their work is so divorced from ordinary life experience? How is it that, especially with large numbers of the modern philosophers, their writings in logic and in the field of knowledge-theory have been more of a closed book to most of us than Einstein's theories of relativity?

Dewey himself has said that the answer lies in "the quest for certainty." That is why Plato sought some Reality behind appearances. That is why the Rock of Ages has been set off against the flux and insecurities of our temporal lives. That is why theory, concerned with ideas (especially mathematical ideas) that are capable of clarity and distinctness, has been thought so superior to practice, with its fuzziness and overlappings. That is why the "blooming, buzzing confusion" of experience has been compared disadvantageously with the quick, clean grasp of Reason.

Yes, in an uncertain, precarious world, men have wanted certainty. And since they could not find it in the world of their experience, they invented another world in which everything could be rationalized or rationally explained, and in which everything we care most about could be thought of as already existing and therefore guaranteed. Actually, it was the philosophers who did this for the run of men. The rank and file sought certainty, but did not know how to find it. The elite thought that they knew how, and since they shared the same need for guarantees as did everyone else, their answers meant that everyone's wishful thinking could be fulfilled. It could be fulfilled, that is, if one man's rationality was not another man's nonsense. Unfortunately, it was. Hence, the major divisions in the great philosophic tradition. But despite differences, there was general agreement about two things: first, that things are not what they appear to be or, indeed, what they are experienced as being; second (this being an intellectual elite, naturally prejudiced in favor of rationality), that the real order of things is a rational order, and once one determines its nature, he can rest secure in the knowledge of it.

There is evidently more in Dewey's analysis than many of

his philosophic colleagues like to admit. They ask, Are certain
propositions advanced by Plato or Descartes or Kant true or false?
If they are false, prove them so; if they are true, build new truth
on them. Instead of which, in large measure, Dewey has offered
historical and psychological explanations of why earlier thinkers
thought as they did. Is it any wonder that, from their point of
view, so many of them have thrown up their hands and said in
effect that, fine gentleman though Dewey is, he simply is not a
philosopher! Dewey, on the other hand, nonchalantly shedding
charges of committing the genetic fallacy, has pressed on toward
the end he has in view. He has been trying to find out what the
theories of different philosophers have *meant*—with the thought
in mind that meaning is wider than truth.

It is obvious that philosophies arise out of the social conditions in which a philosopher lives. Being obvious, the fact has
merited no special attention from most thinkers. But as Justice
Holmes once observed, nothing is so rewarding as a stubborn
examination of the obvious. And when Dewey has declared that
what he regards as the Greek preferences for Reason over experience, for theory over practice, can be closely correlated with
the sharp division between an aristocracy who did the thinking
and a slave class who did the practical work, he has been doing
more than engaging in a polemical tactic. He has been saying
something basic about the meaning of the philosophy itself. He
has been saying that while it was plausible for Greek thinkers to
derogate experience, as he thinks they did, and become the archi-
tects of an unseen world, it is silly for us to do so, since the limiting conditions of their life are fortunately not ours. He has been
saying that, instead of thinking about experience in ways that
have become rutted after two thousand years, we should look at
our experience as freshly as we can, finding out what it means and
then coining the language to express those meanings. Which is
only another way of saying that we have literally to *change* our
minds.

This in itself would be a difficult enough task if the problems
we face were brought on only by the dualistic tradition of the

Greek thinkers. It is not. Modern philosophers, trying to come to grips with the findings of modern physics, gave a new twist to the old problem, and in the course of doing so made a new and especially oppressive problem out of it. It is doubtful if the new problem could have arisen had not the old tradition prevailed. However that may be, the tradition was there, working its way in men's minds, and the new findings were meshed with the old gears. Following Galileo, the physicists found in the course of their experiments that such properties as mass, space, time, and causal relations were always present, but that others were not. In studying falling bodies, for example, it was a matter of indifference whether they were sweet or bitter, hard or soft, red or yellow. The first group of properties were therefore thought of as primary qualities, attaching to bodies themselves. The second group were given a subsidiary status, classified as secondary qualities which were regarded as not being properties of bodies at all, but were somehow "in the mind."

A host of problems created by this distinction, and devices to resolve them, arose in the course of the seventeenth and eighteenth centuries. The most devastating attack of all came from Hume, who suddenly asked, not how the relation between primary and secondary qualities is to be understood, but why any distinction was made between them. All that human beings experience, Hume contended, are sensations, and since the only knowledge we have of primary qualities is our ideas of them, they are "in the mind" in exactly the same way as are secondary qualities. But primary qualities are the only evidence we have that bodies exist. Consequently, the existence of bodies independent of our ideas of them cannot be proved. Furthermore, although for practical purposes we "know" there is a world, in any rigorous sense we have knowledge only of our sensations, and the existence of the world itself is indemonstrable. This is the ultimate paradox of modern philosophy—the inability to prove that which we have to assume in order to be or do anything.

It was this paradox which provoked "the" problem of modern thought, the one above all others to which Kant addressed himself. How is knowledge possible? Now most of us are, in one way or another, concerned with what we mean by knowing something in a specific situation. There is a vast difference between suspecting something is the case and knowing that it is. In an infantile paralysis epidemic, for example, if one's child is suddenly taken with chills and fever, the parent may suspect or fear the worst. But it is impossible to take intelligent steps until one knows. If the fear is groundless, one will take the proper measures to dissipate the fever. If it actually is a case of poliomyelitis, one will immediately get the best treatment available for that dread disease. In this, as in all other life situations, knowledge is both the fruit and the handmaiden of intelligent action. To ask how we can get knowledge in a specific situation, however, is altogether different from asking how knowledge itself, knowledge at large, is possible. This latter question is the springboard of epistemology and, to an almost unbelievable extent, epistemology *is* modern philosophy.

It is on this, and everything implied in it, that Dewey has turned his back. He is concerned with knowledge, to be sure, but concerned with it as the man in the street is concerned. Looked at in one way, it is for him, too, the central problem, yet the way is poles apart from the way of the epistemologists. To understand this it is necessary to understand what he means by nature and experience.

"Nature" is a little word, but it is big in meanings and rich in ambiguities. Etymologically, it has to do with birth, and birth itself is an end as well as a beginning. The life span of any individual is but a moment in the career of the species to which it belongs, yet the species exists only in the lives of the individuals who comprise it. Thus humanity finds a certain fulfillment in the birth of each of us, but death is a warrant that whatever we are is significant primarily in the lives of others. That each of us is, in a profound sense, a child of humanity is no sign that there was anything more mysterious in our conception than the fact itself. And, by the same token, the fact that all life is the offspring of nature does not signify that nature is some strange force or power mysteriously giving life to us. The fact of life is mystery enough, without introducing another mystery into it. In other words, there appears to be no Nature behind nature, which somehow "explains" it. Nor does nature itself "explain" anything else, being nothing but our collective name for existence and its possibilities.

To put the matter differently, nothing could be more natural than whatever is—and if we sometimes think of "unnatural" occurrences or experiences of the "supernatural," that is only another way of saying that something we did not expect has happened. Unless we have been misled by bad metaphysics, we would "naturally" say that our expectation had been wrong, and learn that lesson. The only difficulty here is that such metaphysics themselves sometimes have their origin in our "natural" tendency to overvalue the influence and importance of ideas. "Nature" is whatever happens, and accordingly everything that happens is by definition "natural." As Dewey himself expresses it, illusions are illusions (not to be mistaken for the realities they purportedly present), but when an illusion occurs, it is as much a fact of experience as is anything else. Railroad tracks seem to merge in the distance, and unless we recognized this as an optical illusion, we might build collapsible cars. Obviously, the illusion tells us nothing about railroads. But it does tell us something about vision and perspective, and thus we see that even illusions can be rich in what they suggest about the facts of nature. The only difficulty, always, is to find out just what the facts are. And while we have apparently said something simple in observing that nature is whatever happens, nothing could be more complicated than learning what does happen.

All this has a paradoxical sound, and that is doubtless because nature is as paradoxical as it is fruitful. The paradoxes need detain us, however, only if we have a mind for such sport. If we have not, we can turn to the far more serious and sobering consideration that "nature" is impossible to define. Hence Dewey, for all his laborious efforts to describe the relations of experience and inquiry to nature, has never attempted to define it. Being a realistic Yankee, he probably never gave serious thought to the matter, for the human problem is never to "know" nature at large but to know it specifically, just as one is never engaged in farming in general but in farming a particular tract of land under specific conditions. When we conduct an inquiry into a specific problem, we are engaging in a natural process, and when we have successfully concluded an inquiry, we know that much about nature. When we experience something, say the surf pounding against a rock-bound shore, it is a natural event, and we are experiencing that portion of nature. From the human point of view, accordingly, nature is the sum total of experience—not only what has been experienced and is being experienced but, in addition, whatever may be experienced. And in so far as nature is anything more than this, it is something with which human beings can have literally nothing to do.

To be aware of the limitations both of our knowledge and experience of nature, however, does not leave us islanded in the universe. For human nature is part and parcel of wider nature, and though it is much more than we are, it also is whatever we are. A large part of the difficulty we have in making our way in the world lies in our refusal or inability to see this clearly. That is why various mystic cults, of whom the existentialists are one contemporary example, wring their hands over what they regard as man's fate: to be forever a "stranger" in the universe. From a naturalistic point of view, the ludicrousness of this position is evident as soon as we ask ourselves what it would mean to say that dogs or birds or trees are "strangers" in nature. It is a figure of speech, assuredly, but one that neatly illustrates how far we are from seeing ourselves as genuinely part of nature. Our habits of speech and thinking illustrate the same difficulty in endless ways. Dewey puts the matter concisely when he points out that our breathing is as much an affair of the air as of our lungs. The point is worth pondering. Sitting in a room, if we turn our minds to it, we become conscious of *our* breathing, and nothing would seem sillier to any of us than to think that the *air* is breathing. By breathing, we mean pulling air into our lungs and then expelling it. But suppose the air in the room were some kind of conscious being:

to it, breathing would be a matter of pushing *its* way into some other being's lungs, and then pulling itself out. The illustration may seem not only fanciful but trivial.

If we customarily speak of our being affected by the environment or of our affecting it, however, we should see that this is an oversimplification. For human action taking place in outer nature is always a business of interaction, or, using Dewey's later language, it is a complex of transactions, in which the reciprocal influences are intricately intertwined. When we give priority to either man or nature, accordingly, we are doing so as a matter of convenience or interest, and are not giving an accurate description of the nature of things. If we could only see that every phase of human existence is such a complex of natural relations, we would better understand the relations of experience and nature, and dissipate modern philosophy's conundrum about "proving" that we can have knowledge of the world's existence.

Let us recall how the conundrum arose. We "know" the world only through our experience of it. But do we actually experience "it"? Not at all, said Hume. We experience our sensations, our impressions. Accordingly, experience is "in the mind"; it is subjective. And although we believe in an objective world, we believe in it not because there is any rational progress from the subjective to the objective, but because we indulge in what Santayana has called "animal faith." Furthermore, our sensations themselves are piecemeal, atomic, with no necessary relation between any two of them. In a thunderstorm, one may experience the sensation of lightning, and this may customarily be followed by the sensation of thunder; but our only "reason" for saying that thunder is caused by lightning is our habit of associating the two sensations. This is the root of Hume's skepticism: that causality, which is the existence of necessary relations, is in our experience nothing but the habitual association of impressions. But knowledge depends upon grasping the causal, or necessary, relations of things. It therefore follows that if we can have no experience of necessity, we can have no knowledge.

Kant met the challenge by attempting to show that experience itself is not possible unless it is characterized by such basic categories as causality. He contended that mind, by its very nature, brings these categories to experience, and that they are necessary qualities of any and all experience. In the thinking of many who succeeded him, this was equivalent to saying that mind makes experience what it is, and this became the point of departure for much of modern idealism. Hegelian idealism, as we have seen, took an altogether different approach, insisting that relations, including whatever we mean by necessary relations, are in experience because the Absolute Idea (which includes all experience) is that kind of Absolute. James, who heartily detested the neatly packaged world, the "block universe," of the Absolutists, was really much closer to Hegel on this point than he acknowledged. Experience, he claimed, is not a series of atomistic sensations. On the contrary, we experience relations as much as anything else, and this is because relations themselves are real. This is the nub of James's radical empiricism. Yet he certainly failed to satisfy his critics, who kept hammering away that even if relations are part of experience, experience is still subjective, something that happens inside each of us, and that we are still left with the problem of how the subjective ever "knows" the objective. Although on occasion he was apparently of two minds on this matter, James pretty consistently believed that experience is objective as well as subjective. Had he lived longer, he might have spelled out what he meant. As events turned out, the case for the objective nature of experience was left to Dewey, and in the long run he will be seen as the philosopher of experience as well as of democracy.

It does not detract from the creative work of either James or Dewey to say that they were both immeasurably indebted to that strange genius, Charles Sanders Peirce. Peirce, whose great philosophic contributions have begun to be widely appreciated only in recent years, was so at odds with himself and the world in which he lived that his career was a series of frustrations—indeed, in any professional sense, he had no career at all. Whatever the other causes, one upshot of this was that he never completed any of his work; a reminder to us that even unfinished work, if it is good enough, can reach out beyond the furthest horizons we can see. The son of a noted mathematician, he was himself a mathematician and logician of the first order. And through his effect, not only on James and Dewey, but on such other influential minds as Justice Holmes, Josiah Royce, Morris R. Cohen, and a host of logicians, his ideas are part of the mainstream of American culture, even though most Americans never heard of him and will certainly never read any of his writings.

Born in 1839, he was James's senior by only three years, yet James's characteristic philosophy had its inspiration, if not its base, in some of Peirce's ideas. In the Metaphysical Club which met in Boston in the sixties, and which numbered James, Holmes, and Chauncy Wright (another striking philosophic mind) among its members, Peirce first advanced those basic conceptions that were to be of such far-reaching significance. As much as anything else, it came to an attitude, an approach, to things, an approach that Holmes subsequently applied to the law and that has since helped mold the minds of two generations of American lawyers. In the seventies, Peirce published a series of papers on "How to Make Our Ideas Clear," papers that have proved to be a major contribution to modern thought. Twenty years later, James said that those papers and his many talks with Peirce were the source of his pragmatism. Even though Peirce claimed that James misunderstood him (in some respects he did; in others he was simply expressing James and not Peirce), it is not the first instance in which a misunderstanding has had fruitful results. And when, after still another forty years had passed, Dewey wrote his most comprehensive book on logic, his obligation to Peirce was both apparent and made explicit.

It was Peirce who gave a solid underpinning in modern philosophy to our common-sense acceptance of the world's existence. Modern philosophy had begun with Descartes's declaration that he would doubt everything; but if he doubted, he was thinking, and if he was thinking, he must exist. That much existence, therefore, he could not doubt, and on this basis he purportedly erected his entire philosophy. Peirce showed how specious and how impossible was this attempt to doubt everything and how, under the guise of it, Descartes and others had smuggled into their philosophies things that they had never really doubted, no matter what they thought or said. He enjoined philosophers, accordingly, never to doubt in their thinking what they did not doubt in their hearts. And since, as we have observed, it could never occur to anyone *but* a philosopher to doubt the world's existence, a sensible philosopher is one who will ignore the false problem of "proving" it and will accept its existence as one basis of his thinking. The problem of knowledge is not how it is possible to know anything but how, when we claim we do know something, to determine if it is a valid case of knowledge.

Peirce said that he was aware of only four methods that advanced knowledge-claims. The first is the method of tenacity, of holding on to an idea just because we have it, and insisting that it is a valid case of knowledge because—well, just because it is. The second is the method of authority, of accepting an idea as knowledge because someone we respect or to whom we owe allegiance has said it is true—but that leaves the question of how the someone in authority "knew" it in the first place. The third is the method of intuition, of somehow, suddenly, simply knowing that such and such is the case, as when one looks at a traffic light and "knows" it to be red. But if two people see the same light and one has an intuition that it is red while the other's intuition labels it orange, how is their difference to be settled? Practically, each of these methods comes down to a question of authority and, in the last analysis, the only appeal left to them is the authority of faith or revelation—which is a long way, indeed, from what we mean by knowing something. The fourth method, and the only one that Peirce thought had any reliability, is the method of science. Here is his basic relation to Dewey. For scientific method involves part of what Dewey means by experience, and everything he means by knowledge. We shall therefore have to examine it in somewhat more detail.

Dewey, with Peirce and James, accepts the common-sense

fact of the world's existence. With them, too, he accepts the basic premise that experience is no more subjective than objective. The case of breathing is a prime example of what he means. The same thing holds for every phase of experience: walking is as much an affair of the ground as of our legs, eating inescapably involves food as much as it does our digestive systems, seeing means something to be seen and not merely our eyes—and exactly so with the whole gamut of experience and our sensory equipment in relation to it. We are biological organisms functioning in the world in which we find ourselves, and when we have experiences of touching, tasting, smelling, or hearing, it means that *things* are being touched, tasted, smelled, or heard. These considerations are so commonplace that it seems ridiculous to most people (until they are confounded by dialectic) that Dewey or anyone else should labor them. In the philosophic tradition, however, this commonsenseism has been labeled "naïve realism," and essentially the condemnation of it rests on the proposition that things are not what they appear to be. Fortunately for the health of modern philosophy, the idea that things exist independently of our experiencing them—which is the modern meaning of realism—has had wide support, and thinkers as different from Dewey as Santayana, Whitehead, and Russell have been at one with him about this.

For Dewey, the matter goes further, and he would agree with James and the little-known nineteenth-century English philosopher Shadworth Hodgson that things *are* what they are experienced as being, what they are known as, though it is essential to understand that he does not mean they are whatever at first blush they appear to be nor only what they are experienced as being. In his view, it would be fantastic to accept Hume's dictum that we experience sensations. Hume's whole position rests on a faulty psychology. If we say that we are experiencing sensations, what are they sensations *of?* Of other sensations? No, we have sensations of things or objects, and when we say we have a sensation of lightning, we are experiencing not the sensation but the lightning. Of course, it may be said that we can have the sensation of lightning without there being any, as when hit over the head by a club or when having an hallucination. Evidently, however, this is not a question of what experience is; it is again a question of knowledge. As James pointed out, mental fire is what won't burn real wood—and, to reverse the point of view, real lightning is what will destroy a house or set fire to a tree or kill a human being.

Experience is not "in the mind." It is both inner and outer, something happening in the world as well as in ourselves. We see once more, accordingly, that the human problem is not the specious one of proving the world's existence or the question of whether, granted there is a world, we can experience it. The problem is to determine what is happening, when we put our minds to it, and of having some kind of security that if we say, "My pipe is now burning because I lit the tobacco with a match," we know what we are talking about.

Now "knowledge" is at least as complicated a word as is "experience." It has so many different meanings, and suggests so many different kinds of experience to so many different people, that it becomes supremely difficult to have any meeting of minds. We often say, for example, "I know that man from A to Z"— meaning that we think we can anticipate his behavior, that we have insight into his strengths and weaknesses, with special emphasis on the weaknesses. Or we say, "Yes, I know Mary Thompson. I met her at the Smiths' a short time ago"—meaning that we are slightly acquainted with her. Or we say, "I know it's going to rain tomorrow as surely as I know my own name"—meaning that we do not know it at all. Or we say, "I've listened to that Mozart Quintet a dozen times in the last week, and I think I'm finally beginning to know it"—meaning, among other things, that we have a certain feeling of at-homeness with it. Or we say, "If you've ever been in the Finger Lakes region, then you know that the sunsets are something out of this world"—meaning that we have experienced their beauty for ourselves. Or we say, "To know anything at all about plane geometry is to know that the square of the hypotenuse of a right-angled triangle is equal to the sum of the squares of the other two sides"—meaning that in a mathematical system, certain things necessarily follow from certain others. Or we say, "It occurred to me that if hydrogen and oxygen are combined under certain conditions in the ratio of two parts to one, water will result. I have tried this a number of times, and I understand that under similar conditions a number of other people have tried it. And every time, water did result. Therefore, I conclude that my hypothesis was a sound one, and I know that water is $H_2O$"—meaning that a proposition has been experimentally verified under certain conditions which warrant our accepting it.

Numbers of other illustrations could be given to show various other ways in which "knowing" is understood in common usage. For our present purposes, the important point is that only the last case, of experimental verification or scientific method, is what Dewey means by "knowing." This is not due to any arbitrariness on his part—except the arbitrariness of saying that if words are to be used intelligibly, they have to be defined as precisely as possible. It is due rather to the profound insight, which he shares with Peirce and James, that knowledge has to do with the relatively dependable consequences of activity.

This attitude toward knowledge, as an active relation between persons and things, has been responsible for as many misunderstandings, and as much pointless verbiage, as any other one subject in contemporary philosophy. Let us first see what Dewey is saying, so that we can better see what this means.

Suppose we wish to boil some eggs and the friend in whose home we are staying says, "Here's a pot of water. Use this." But we have many times experienced this friend's practical jokes, and we suspect that once more he is trying to victimize us. We look at him skeptically and ask, "Is it really water? Or is it some kind of acid that will dissolve the eggs?" He responds, "Try it yourself if you don't believe me. Then you'll know!"

Here is a typical knowledge-situation. How are we to find out what it is? Obviously, we cannot tell by looking at it, since any one of a number of other things might look like water. Obviously, too, we cannot tell anything conclusive by sniffing it, since a number of other things that look like water might also be odorless. One thing we can do is sip it, and if it affects our taste buds and gullets the way water ordinarily does, we shall probably say, "I think it is water, all right." Our devilish friend has us on the run, however, and with a glint in his eye he caustically remarks, "Oho, you *think* it is! You didn't trust me in the first place, and you haven't given it much of a test. Why don't you make sure?" "All right, I will," is our acceptance of the challenge. But how? Then we remember that water boils at 212° Fahrenheit and ask our friend for a thermometer. We place it in the pot of liquid, light the gas under it, and the moment it starts to boil, withdraw the thermometer. If the reading actually is 212°, we are likely to be convinced, and to observe, "Well, at least I *know* now that it is water."

Now let us examine what has happened. In order to get the knowledge we needed, we went through several operations involving the water as much as ourselves, as related parts of one experience. First, we sipped it; and of course, the amount we sipped was no longer in the pot but in us. Next, we heated it until it boiled and some of it started to steam away. It was at this point that we confessed we "knew." Evidently, though, the boiling water that we finally know is somewhat different from the cold liquid we started out to know.

This commonplace fact, which would never give anybody any pause whatever in his ordinary life, has been the focal point of endless philosophic dispute. Trying to describe this knowledge-experience as accurately as he can, Dewey has insisted that the object of knowledge (the boiling water) was not "there" before we started our tests; or, to use his terminology, the object of knowledge is not an "antecedent reality." This is not to deny that there was some kind of liquid in a pot (if we ask how we "knew" it was liquid, we would have to go through operations appropriate to determining *that*), a liquid we thought might or might not be water. If there had not been, there would have been neither a problem nor the necessity of resolving it. It is simply to affirm that we *knew* it was water only after we had tested (transformed) it. This commonplace has been the object of much hilarity and ridicule from philosophers of differing schools. They charge Dewey with never being able to know what he started out to know, but always something different. Then they ask indignantly what kind of "knowledge" it is that can never hit what it is aiming at!

"By their fruits ye shall know them," the Bible cautions us— and one wonders why more philosophers have not pondered the saying. A cowpuncher knows his horse after he has broken him in, ridden him for hours, and trained him to behave in certain ways. A farmer knows his soil is fertile when it yields a good crop. A mechanic knows an automobile motor is in good condition after he has put it through certain tests. And so on, up and down the line of our experience. Some philosophers may derive a kind of satisfaction out of "confounding" Dewey, but in our daily lives most of the rest of us realize that we know something only as the result of adequate testing.

The whole controversy would not be worth the paper it is written on, except as an intellectual exercise, did it not have implications of the broadest importance. Who but a philosopher cares whether the object of knowledge is an "antecedent reality"? The answer is that, whether we are aware of it or not, the outcome of the issue matters a great deal to all of us. Philosophers, religious leaders, educators, and others have assured the human race for so many centuries that our daily practices have nothing to do with Reality, Truth, and Knowledge, that countless millions of people have always been cowed by them and continue to be cowed by them today. What is the upshot of it? This attitude provides the intellectual basis for authoritarian and totalitarian movements of every kind. It is the chief instrument for the mass control of men's minds. If a given church claims to be the sole custodian of the Truth, by virtue of faith and revelation, how is its claim to be vindicated or refuted? By a clash of authorities, a sheer power struggle, such as we witness in our time between Catholicism and communism? If a Hitler claims he "knows" that the German people, and they alone, are fit to be the master race of humanity, by virtue of his intuitions, can the claim be settled only by the destruction of thirty million lives? If a Cominform claims that it alone can lead the way to "the people's democracy" because it is the keeper of the Marxist gospel propounded by Lenin and edited by Stalin, can the claim be answered only by the atom bomb? No, to use Peirce's classifications, the methods of tenacity, of authority, of intuition are not the methods of knowledge of a genuinely educated and civilized people. The method of testing, of controlled experimentation, with results open to challenge by anyone, anywhere, at any time, this is the only method of knowledge fit for a mature and free people.

That is why Dewey has persistently placed so much emphasis on disposing of the "antecedent-reality" fiction in the knowledge-process. It is the wedge of the dualistic bugaboo which he regards as the besetting sin of the philosophic tradition—splitting the world into separate compartments of mind and matter, subject and object, experience and nature, knowledge and reality, and then devising various subtle ways of putting it together again. Most of the ways have terminated in some person's or some group's authoritative deliverances. But the scientific method is the democratic method.

We can now better understand why Dewey could not attempt to define nature at large, as well as the sense in which things are what they are experienced as being. Nature is bigger, broader, deeper, thicker, than we know it to be, but it also is whatever we know it to be. When we say we know a particular part of nature, we mean that we have engaged in certain operations which led to certain results. And the results we thus experience *are* that much of nature.

It may be asked, however, how we can be *sure* about our results, for just such certainty has been traditionally taken as the sign of knowledge. The answer is, we cannot be sure—and yet these results comprise our knowledge. To return to our illustration of the boiling water, we can imagine that under some circumstances we would not be satisfied with the thermometer experiment. For all we know, other things that look like water might have a boiling point of 212°. We might then take the pot of liquid to another friend's laboratory, asking him to subject it to the test of electrolysis, and find that it separated into two parts hydrogen and one part oxygen. But we still could not be absolutely sure that only water, of all possible liquids, reacts in this way. After we sipped it, we believed that the liquid was probably water; after we boiled it, our belief was greatly strengthened; after we separated it into hydrogen and oxygen, the probability of its being water was so great that neither we nor most other people would be inclined to doubt it. In other words, the methods of science never yield certainty. The high degree of probability of its results, however, has enabled us to transform the earth. The philosopher F. J. E. Woodbridge once remarked that if this is not knowledge, he would like to see a sample of the real article. Those of us not already beguiled by the alternative methods of "knowledge" are likely to agree with him. For no matter how much we may differ with Marx's political and economic views, we probably accord with his observation that the problem of knowledge is not simply to understand the world, but to change it. It is in the context of a dynamic, changing world that Dewey has always regarded ideas as instruments, which is why his philosophy has sometimes been labeled "instrumentalism."

Ideas have been thought of in a variety of ways. One is to regard them as mental copies of the realities they represent, as when we have an idea of a person we love and "picture" that person to ourselves; or to regard them as somehow corresponding to realities or agreeing with them, as when the lines on a graph "correspond" to the ups and downs of sales and prices on the stock market. On the basis of this theory, we say an idea is true if it is an accurate copy or if the correspondence is genuine and reliable. But how are we to know if a copy *is* accurate; what criterion can we use for genuineness and reliability? In other words, this conception of ideas promises more than it delivers, for in any specific situation we are left with the problem of determining, somehow, whether an idea is sound or unsound, true or false.

In the last analysis, according to Dewey, the difficulty comes down to a misconception of what ideas are. To regard them as "copies" of reality or "agreements" with it is to regard ourselves as spectators in a world in which things happen, instead of as active participants in the happenings. This, in turn, is due to the traditional dualisms between mind and matter, experience and nature, appearance and reality. Having disposed of these dualisms, we are in a position to tackle the question of ideas afresh, by asking in what kinds of situations they arise and what functions they are called upon to perform.

Ideas have their origin in doubtful situations. It is important to realize that in such cases it is not simply a person who is in doubt. The situations themselves are doubtful, or indeterminate. It was Woodrow Wilson who said that nothing was more inaccurate than for a person lost in the woods to say that he was lost; on the contrary, he knew where *he* was all right, but he did not know where anything else was in relation to himself. The point that is made is more than a play on words, as we can see by returning momentarily to our problem of boiling eggs. From one point of view, we can say that the liquid in the pot was water all the time. There was nothing doubtful about that. It was we who were in doubt about whether to use it. But this does not describe the existing situation, for it takes the liquid and us separately, out of context. The actual situation was not a pot of water on the one hand and ourselves on the other. The situation was: We-wish-to-boils-eggs-in-a-pot-of-liquid-which-may-be-water-or-may-be-acid. This *situation* was doubtful.

Now in all such doubtful situations, we are compelled to take thought—compelled, that is, if we cannot ignore them and they inhibit our continued activity. Psychologically, the experience for us may be one of mild annoyance or of concern or of anxiety, depending upon the seriousness of the situation. In such a predicament, one way or another, we get a suggestion, a hunch, an intuition about what is involved. When this has happened, we have already progressed from an indeterminate situation to one in which we can begin to focus on the problem implicit in it.

For example, a man may sit down to dinner one evening, just as he does every other evening, but feeling annoyed for some reason he does not understand. Then he realizes that ever since he walked into the house his wife has seemed distant, by no means a usual thing. He puzzles about this (indeterminate situation)— and then it dawns on him. This is her birthday, and he has forgotten all about it. *Now* he has a problem! Once he comes face to face with this, he can begin to go to work on what is to be done. He may turn various possibilities over in his mind. Should he pretend that he has not forgotten the birthday at all, but all along has been planning a surprise for her—later by some pretext leaving the house for a few minutes, in the desperate hope that he can garner theater tickets for that night? Should he say, apologetically, that her gift was to have been delivered to his office so that he could bring it home to her, but that the store had failed him? Or should he make a clean breast of it, confess his absent-mindedness, in the hope that he will be able to make amends for it? "Yes, that's it," he may say to himself, "an honest confession is the best idea." And, in Dewey's terms, as against his earlier confusion and sudden insight, he now genuinely has what can be called an idea—that is, a proposal for something he can do to resolve the problem. Strictly speaking, of course, each of the other possibilities he turned over in his mind, only to be dismissed, was also an idea in just this sense.

What is the test of whether it is a good or sound idea? In a situation of this kind, the answer is obvious. It was a good idea if it actually did resolve the problem it was devised to meet. And, if it did, we can say that we knew how to act in that situation, that we are in possession of that much knowledge. Some of us might be inclined to generalize from the experience and to say that in all intimate personal relations, an honest confession of guilt is the best way to deal with problems of this kind. Here we push further with Dewey in our understanding of scientific method. We have to determine, in a second situation, if it really does involve the same kind of problem as the first, and that requires careful observation, analysis, comparison, judgment. If it does, if the problems are of the same kind, we can then employ our generalization, which has become our guiding principle of action. We cannot be sure that it will solve the problem this time. A successful result again would strengthen the generalization, give us more confidence in it. An unsuccessful result might lead us to re-examine the whole situation, in an effort to find out what had gone wrong. Finding no mistakes in judgment or in application of the principle, we would be forced either to modify it or abandon it.

The use of scientific method in dealing with human problems has been Dewey's major emphasis, and we shall return to the question. For the moment, let us bear in mind that it is a considerably more complex matter than the use of the method in astronomy, physics, or chemistry, and that while we have begun to see what it means, we are only at the beginning. In the highly developed physical sciences, mathematics or deductive logic plays an essential part in the entire process.

One of the most graphic illustrations of this may be found in the development of the relativity theory. At the end of the nineteenth century, physicists were confronted with certain facts that could not be satisfactorily accounted for on the principles formulated by Newton. They might question the facts, which seemed undeniable. Or they might question the principles, which had been verified countless times over two centuries. It was an uncomfortable, not to say chaotic, situation. But it was a situation that had to be faced. Some of them faced it by re-examining the facts. Einstein faced it by questioning the principles.

Let us assume, Einstein said in effect, that Newton's principles are valid for one class of facts, but are not valid for a wider class. Let us assume, further, that principle $X$ (later called the theory of relativity) is valid for this wider class. But how are we to verify principle $X$? There are no experiments that will directly either substantiate or refute it. The next step, therefore, involved no experiments at all. It was all paper work, straight mathematics. If $X$, $Y$ follows from it; if $Y$, then $Z$; if $Z$, then $A$. In other words, $A$ necessarily follows from $X$, and if $X$ is true, $A$ is true. Now among the consequences of $X$ are principles of a general character, like $X$ itself, and other types of consequences that point to things that can be observed or subjected to experiment. $A$ is one of the latter we *can* verify, it is an experiment we can perform. And if we have a successful result, it will reflect credit on the principle $X$ from which we derived or predicted it mathematically. So the experiment with $A$—carefully controlled observation of a distant star when it is eclipsed by a planet—is conducted, $A$ is verified, and $X$ (the theory of relativity) is accordingly on its way to confirmation. The important consideration at the moment is that the theory, on its mathematical basis alone, made a good deal of sense to the physicists who understood it, and it was part of their approach to problems for some years before it was experimentally verified.

It is in the light of such experience as this that many students of scientific method charge Dewey with overemphasizing experimentation and undervaluing mathematics, with giving too much importance to inductive and not enough to deductive logic. It is a serious charge, but it is more apparent than real. For as Dewey sees it, the manipulation of mathematical symbols on a sheet of paper is no less an operation, no less an experiment, than is the use of equipment in a laboratory. The point for him is that they are two different kinds of operations, each in its own way involving our active relation to the world in which we live.

Let us remember, however, that we are trying to determine the nature and function of ideas. In a nutshell, they are proposals for action, whether in connection with our day-to-day problems or in the more carefully organized pursuits of science. Nor is a scientifically validated idea any more of an idea than one we use in our daily practices. Neither is it a different kind of idea. In each case, furthermore, the test of an idea's validity is the consequences of it. It is valid if it solves the problem that called it forth. The results of such problem solving constitute knowledge. But again, ideas are not separate from knowledge. They are links in the same chain, parts of the same process. "Knowledge" is simply our shorthand expression for the whole process, starting with the indeterminate situation, and going on through the formulation of

the problem, the getting of a hunch for its solution, the canvass-
ing of that hunch's various implications, and its experimental
verification.

Thinking begins in a doubtful situation and its aim is the re-
moval of doubt. It was Peirce who first stressed that the consequences of inquiry were accordingly the important aspect of it,
the most important consequences to his mind being general principles that would be fruitful in further forwarding inquiry. James,
with his impatience with the general and his love for the specific,
the particular person and the particular thing, believed that the
important consequences were those that led to the particular thing
we are aiming at. Primarily, this is the difference between the
pragmatism of Peirce and James. Dewey has compounded the
two. For him, knowledge that is not for human use is of no use
at all (except for the satisfactions gained in achieving and possessing it), but the only handles to such knowledge are valid general principles. Physical tools can help us deal with specific problems, as a lever will move a boulder we cannot otherwise budge,
but general principles are the tools for making tools. It is in this
sense that ideas are instrumental, the necessary tools for solving
problems and achieving knowledge.

It will be noted that so far in this discussion of ideas we have
spoken of them as sound or unsound, valid or invalid. What about
truth? Essentially, we are accustomed to speaking of ideas as true
or false. Why does Dewey not speak of them this way? The answer
takes us back to the dualism between appearance and reality, and
to the difference between the conceptions of a static and a changing universe. In the dualistic tradition, Reality and Truth were
one and the same, unchanging and eternal. A true idea, therefore,
was one that "corresponded" to this Reality, grasped this Truth,
apprehended this Essence. But in a changing universe, this my-
thology must be seen for what it is. In a developing nature, problems themselves change, and knowledge changes with them. And
in our efforts to solve whatever problems confront us, the question is not so much whether ideas are true or false, but whether
they are relevant or irrelevant, effective or ineffective, valid or in-

valid. "Truth" is a word so overladen with traditional metaphysics that to use it would incur the risk of beclouding the whole issue. So instead of using it, Dewey has come to the point of saying that an idea that is found valid in inquiry is one we are "warranted" in accepting, one we can "assert" with confidence—"truth" thereby becoming "warranted assertibility." His reasons for using this barbarous term should be evident, but it remains a barbarism, and an unwieldy one at that. If it does not come into common usage, it will not be cause for regret.

Having come this far in our survey of what nature, experience, and knowledge mean for Dewey, we can ask ourselves what, for him, is the nature of the world we live in. First, it is a real world, one in which experience is as real as anything else. Second, it is a world of change, spawning problems time without end. Third, it is a world in which ideas, too, are real, for they are our chief handles to the solving of problems. And if we ask, But what, specifically, do we know about the nature or character of the world?, Dewey cannot give the encyclopedic response required. We must turn to the accumulated results of the special sciences for that, realizing that tomorrow we shall know more than we do today, and hoping that a hundred years from now our present knowledge will seem infinitesimally scant. And then we have to remind ourselves that knowledge itself is only a portion of experience, by no means the most important.

Everything that we mean by the goods of life—the beauty, the joys, the creations and achievements, the fulfillments, the sharings—and everything that we mean by the "bads" of it—the failures and frustrations, the cruelties and stupidities, the heartaches and the sufferings—all these things that give meaning to life, these are experience in its full breadth and thickness. Because Dewey has given so much of his attention to the knowledge-process, and because knowledge for him always involves some kind of practice and practicality, he is constantly accused of being a "materialist" who justifies our worst money-grubbing activities, cheapening and coarsening the finest things in life. The charge, in one form or another, has come from some of his most distinguished contemporaries, who see his philosophy as nothing but an expression of a dollar-minded and machine-driven culture. Well, they may have read his books, but they do not understand them—perhaps one reason why philosophic controversies sometimes seem so endless and pointless. No, the scathing denunciations Dewey has written about these very "materialist" aspects of our common life are ample refutation. Knowledge is practical, to be sure, but its aim is no cheap "practicality." In a changing, precarious world, where no one can guarantee what tomorrow may bring, the goods of life are as precarious as anything else, and their very precariousness is what gives human existence its greatest poignancy. The human problem is to make these goods as stable as we can, to insure them to the fullest extent. That is the function of knowledge. And if, in the light of this, we ask again, "What is the nature of the world we live in?", Dewey will refer us to painting, sculpture, music, literature, architecture, drama— for the savor of experience and of nature is best found in the arts.

CHAPTER THREE

# THE POSSIBILITIES OF HUMAN
# NATURE

HUMAN nature is wondrous in many ways, not the least of which are the ways in which it can think and talk about itself. It is good or evil, changing or unchanging, clean or corrupt, reasonable or emotional, promising or perverse, sacred or vile. With the shifting of the social winds and tides, each emphasis seems almost to be a matter of vogue, with now this virtue and now that vice in fashion. An objective mind might view this curious careening with amusement, if not with tolerance, were not such important issues at stake. But they are at stake—and what we think about what we are has more than a little to do with what we are to become.

Nowadays, some "serious" thinkers seem to be very down on human nature, to be selling it short. They are condescending toward what they call the easy optimism of an earlier day, and sometimes downright contemptuous of it. Why is it, one is forced to ask, that for so many of these thinkers optimism is always "easy" and "sentimental," pessimism always "hard" and "realistic"? Grown to maturity in a barbarous age, such pundits and prophets fancy themselves of sterner stuff, ready to accept the "fact" of man's corruption and sinfulness. It is not enough for them that human beings in our time live with a burden of anxiety. No, indeed; this commonplace must be given a metaphysical status, a place in the inner structure of the universe. The anxiety with which we are all familiar thereby becomes for them the *Angst* before which we are all to bow down.

Sociologically, historically, this is not difficult to understand, although the movement of men's minds always has some unanalyzable surd in it. The invention of progress, with endless testimonials in physical science and industrial technology, was for many years regarded as applying almost mechanically to human beings as well. Man had advanced from the horse-drawn carriage to the steam locomotive, from the locomotive to the dynamo, from the dynamo to the gasoline engine, from the engine to nuclear energy. He had moved from literal manu-facture to mass production, from feudalism to industrialism, from a society of status to one of opportunity, from aristocracy to democracy. Why should he not, then, advance the kingdom of heaven itself, moving it up from an unseen afterworld to the world of here and now? Why should not the Christian gospel become a social gospel, with human eyes fixed not on some eternal perfection but on temporal perfectibility? The answer for many people was almost self-evident: it should be, it could be, and it was.

Then came the nightmare years, in which the era of good feeling was shredded and shrouded. In retrospect, the horrors of World War I seemed almost like a harmonious prelude, a colorful intimation of the cataclysmic twilight of the gods. First the world goose-stepped and trembled before the comically grim little man in Berlin. Next it gaped, beyond nausea, at Buchenwald and Dachau. Then it found ruthless oppression blithely called "the people's democracy." And finally it looked upon the atom bomb as an intelligent means of defense.

It is no wonder, in this through-the-looking-glass world, that old myths crept out of hiding to be accepted as new realities. Everyone of any sensitivity felt somehow dirtied by what the world was, tainted by a sense of guilt which was no less pervasive because it was so often unavowed. "There, but for the grace of God, go I," it was once remarked when a criminal was seen being marched to the gallows. Now the saying was generalized and, however subconsciously, the bestiality of other people was seen as one's own possible lot. But for the grace of God! That was it, and the theologians began to have their field day. The trouble with humanity is its secularism, its failure to have a consciousness of God in daily activities, one hierarchy assured us. The trouble with humanity is its essential corruption, the fact of original sin to which we have tragically blinded ourselves, another group of religious thinks averred. The trouble with humanity is that it is human, they agreed. And our only hope lies in the intervention of God's grace, whether through one churchly institution or another—which one they could not agree. Faith in intelligence is a snare, and faith in people a delusion. What we are is what we always have been and always will be: poor creatures struggling against our own evil natures; or, if we prefer the accents of the neo-orthodox, creatures haunted by the cosmic precariousness of our existence, desperately seeking to salvage hope even out of the hopeless odds against us.

The strange part of it is that these pessimistic religious views of human nature have something basic in common with the optimistic materialist views of communism. Where the one speaks of man's essential evil, the other speaks of his essential goodness, attributing all evil to economic institutions. Where the one speaks of religious the other speaks of political salvation, each to be achieved in equally miraculous ways. Where one speaks of spirit the other speaks of science, but they are brothers in dogmatism. And however divergent the ways, each is convinced that his is *the* way to *the* truth in a world in which *this* is what human beings are.

Where, in all this, is the infinite richness and variety of human nature?

The fallacy common to all these attitudes, whatever their distinguishing differences, is the assumption that human nature is somehow "given." For them, it is what it is, and there is a persisting core which dictates what man has to be. It is evident that, in Dewey's terms, this assumption is just one more manifestation of the quest for certainty—the need for an unchanging Reality to which we can anchor ourselves in a world of seeming flux. By the same token, it manifests the dualistic emphasis of the tradition: for it pits the "rational" against the "emotional," the "good" against the "evil," the "spiritual" against the "animal" man. And having created these almost unbridgeable gaps between different aspects of man's "nature," it requires some kind of miracle to bridge them. Needless to say, in this as in other respects the philosophic and theological traditions have been as inventive in producing these miracles as in creating the difficulties that required them.

If we start from another assumption, however, we are led to altogether different conclusions. Let us assume that there is no original datum called Human Nature which, through the ages, is an endless series of copies of the first creation. Let us assume, instead, that what we lump together as human nature is a conglomeration of processes, just as is the rest of nature, processes of discovery and creation, of action and interaction, of tension and intention. We see, first, that it cannot be described in fixed categories, because it is not fixed. We see, second, that at any moment in the historic movement of events human nature cannot altogether say what it is, simply because it has no adequate idea of its possibilities, of what it can be. And we see, third, that we have to ask ourselves what makes human nature what it is at any given time—reminding ourselves of Shaw's witticism that if human nature never changed, we would still be climbing around in the trees.

In effect, these are the assumptions Dewey makes, justifying them, not dogmatically, but by an appeal to our ongoing experience. When he asks what makes us what we are, he finds the answer in the organization of society, in the culture to which we belong. Human nature is not merely the adaptation of a biological organism to the environment in which it finds itself. One of its distinguishing characteristics, on the contrary, is that it can adapt the environment to itself. In a measure, it creates its environment, and in doing so, it creates itself. Nor is the environment nothing but the physical world of sun and rain, trees and mountains, rivers and deserts, growth and decay. It is a human environment as well, consisting of people and their products—or, to speak more technically, of the artifacts and institutions that comprise a culture.

An infant is the creature of its environment, making demands upon it, to be sure, but helpless to enforce them. As it develops, it gains a measure of control over its environing conditions: in its ability to manipulate things physically, and even more in the ability to manipulate its parents psychologically. What happens in the process is that a person is being created (the process ends only when life does); and we see developing before our eyes this specific bit of human nature.

Just so does human nature as a whole, as a collection of all the individuals who are "expressions" of it, develop and create itself. Accordingly, when we say that although individuals vary, human nature itself never changes, we are looking at life nearsightedly, without sufficient perspective. It is like saying that although the water of a river constantly changes, the banks endure. Relatively, of course, they do endure, or there could be no river. But the changing geography of the globe is testimony enough to the fact that they do not endure in the same way forever. To continue with the figure, "human nature" is the banks of the stream of human life, and while its rate of change is slower than the passage of individuals and generations, change it assuredly does.

This point is so important, and so central to Dewey's thinking, that it is worth our spending a little more time on it. Curiously enough, those who contend that human nature never really or basically changes are themselves divided into two camps separated by a universe of thought and attitude. On the one side are the conservatives who fall into two groups: the religious traditionalists insist that man's essential nature is his God-given soul, while the cynical "realists" or "materialists" insist that civilization is a veneer thinly covering our essential brutishness. On the other side are the radicals, whether the social revolutionary variety with their economic emphasis or the orthodox Freudians who stress the centrality of the pleasure principle or sex.

The general approach of the conservatives, on its best level, is familiar enough to be commonplace. Try to tell them that human nature changes, and they are likely to respond: "What do you mean, it changes! Do you think greed among us is any different from what it was when Jesus drove the money-changers from the temple! Was Napoleon's ambition of a different kind from that of Alexander the Great! Are lust and licentiousness anything else today than what they were in ancient Rome! Is a jealous lover today experiencing anything essentially different from what a jealous lover in Elizabethan England experienced! Were Nazi terror and bestiality not the same as the terror and bestiality of Genghis Khan and Attila's Huns! Believe me, down at the bottom human nature never changes at all!"

There is so much seeming soundness in this attitude that for many people it is self-evident and unanswerable. And there is a great deal more in our common experience that appears to give added support to it. The stories in the Bible, the tragedies of Aeschylus and Sophocles, the poems of Horace and Catullus, the confessions of St. Augustine, all these and untold numbers of other expressions of the human spirit speak somehow in a language that makes sense to us. We can feel part of what they felt, know part of what they knew, even "see" part of what they saw. In a word, the human in us responds to the human in them, and we say that we "understand" them. But how could this be if their human nature were different from ours? It is only because of our essential sameness that one age can speak to another.

Then we shift our perspective a bit, and think of Edwin Arlington Robinson's sensitive poetic tribute to Shakespeare. In the course of it, Ben Jonson is made to remark of his gigantic contemporary that he peoples Rome "with timeless Englishmen." What is there about the observation that arrests us, that appears on reflection to be so profoundly true? It is the knowledge that no person, not even Shakespeare, can completely transcend the time in which he lives: that his Hamlet, Caesar, Cleopatra, or Richard the Third are not the figures who lived in historic times (as we should not expect them to be), but projections to other imaginative places and times of what the playwright was experiencing in the English Renaissance.

Perhaps, as Aristole said, poetry is truer than history. Whatever validity the saying has, however, lies in his using the word "truth" ambiguously, in two completely different ways. The difference is vital to our present discussion. For the "truth" of human nature as Shakespeare or any other great artist depicts it comes from the abstraction of certain elements in experience which are in turn concretely re-created. This does not happen in time-succession in an artist's mind, but it does happen in fact. The "truth" of human nature as it shows itself historically is in an altogether different dimension. Obviously, since history as it occurs is beyond all possibility of being contained in history as it is written, the historian, too, abstracts certain elements and experiences, attempting to re-create them with his equivalent of their original concreteness. It is not in the process of creation or re-creation, therefore, that the historian differs from the artist. It is rather in the intent. And when we commonly speak of art as timeless, we are putting our finger on just the point of difference in intention. Great art is timeless not merely in the sense that it will never die. Even more importantly, it is timeless in that the historic sequence of events, with a so-called historical novel as well as with other creations, has nothing to do with what it is aiming at.

Let us be more specific. Take the case of Caesar seeing the pyramids of Egypt for the first time, and imagine, respectively, an "artistic" and a "historical" approach to the situation. For a dramatist, Caesar might soliloquize about the vanity of human ambition, and wonder aloud if his own ceaseless upward struggle would end only in the piling of stone upon stone. There would be a "timeless" truth about human nature in this presentation, having nothing to do with the Roman conquest of Egypt. For a historian, however, lacking documents that recorded the conqueror's actual thoughts, the scene might present itself as one in which Caesar took stock of his possibilities; having now mastered the granaries of the Nile valley, should he make his capital at Byzantium in-

stead of Rome, thus opening the way to the conquest of the Orient
and the mastery of the entire world?

Now neither the dramatist nor the historian "knows" what
was going on in Caesar's mind. For our present purposes, the
point is that the dramatist finds historical conditions relevant to
his purpose only as they provide the setting, the backdrop and
atmosphere, for the mood he is eager to create. For the historian,
on the other hand, these cultural conditions are part of the very
problem he has posed for himself, they are central to the questions he is trying to answer, they are indispensable tools of understanding. Indeed, regardless of how much "human nature" Caesar
shares with others in the artistic creation, the historical Caesar
could be confronted only by the problems with which his culture
confronted him. We can go further and say that the Romans
of Caesar's day were expressing their human nature through the
institutions of their culture: the patterns of family life, the instruments of law and politics, the methods of production and distri-
bution of goods, the relations of social classes. Then we can take
the last step and say that, in any concrete sense, there was no
Roman human nature apart from these institutions. We shall
have to come back to a more detailed examination of this
point.

For the moment, let us remind ourselves that for all the
"timelessness" of artistic creations, and the degree to which
human nature thus depicted appears unchanging because of it,
both the artist and his work are creatures of their time. Just as
with Shakespeare, so every creator projects the experience of his
culture. It ought to be evident that the deeper we penetrate into
the culture in which a given work of art was created, the greater
becomes our understanding of it. Which brings us face to face with
the limitation or final frustration of our understanding in all such
matters: that the ways in which one culture differs from another
are so subtle and pervasive that there are areas forever closed to
one who is not a member of it.

We can see, then, that the so-called constancy of human
nature claimed by the conservatives depends upon an abstraction

of certain elements of experience and a dogmatizing about them. There follows the specious security of "knowing" what human nature *really* is, no matter what the guises in which it presents itself. The only trouble is that such understanding may give us some insights into the nature of human nature, but it tells us singularly little about the ways in which people actually behave. Justice Holmes once remarked that the life of the law lies not in logic but in experience. Just so does human nature find itself, not in a series of abstractions, however cogent, but in the precarious concreteness of every individual life.

Nor is the situation essentially different with the radicals, for they, too, abstract certain elements of experience and dogmatize about them. This is evident in the thinking of some of the earlier Freudians. Freud himself was undoubtedly one of the greatest psychologists of all time, and his approach to problems of human nature was one of the most radical in the history of thought. Out of his investigations of personal problems, he came to the conclusion that what he called the Oedipus complex—the incestuous love of a son for his mother, and its obverse in the case of daughter and father—was a characteristic of human development. The behavior profile of an individual could be sketched in terms of it: whether in the passage from childhood to adulthood he remained in this web or successfully passed beyond it to other levels of emotional attachment.

The earlier investigations carried on by psychoanalysts seemed to give confirmation to this hypothesis. Then other scientists called attention to the fact that these investigations had been carried on among people who belonged to Western cultures (western Europe and America) and were overwhelmingly members of the middle class. It is by no means demonstrated that even in Western culture those who have not been raised in the pattern of middle-class family life experience the same kind of development or that the pattern is validated for those who have. And it is still more doubtful that the theory of the Oedipus complex has anything at all to do with persons whose culture is not built around the monogamous family. To say that the classic Oedipal situation is an essential handle to the understanding of human nature, accordingly, is simply a dogma, as unwarranted by the available evidence as dogmatism always is.

More serious in its implications than this, however, and more relevant to our present discussion, is the Freudian thesis that the pleasure principle is central to human development. Because Freud stated his case in terms of sex, starting out with infant sexuality, his original reception was one of outrage and abuse. What kind of monster was he who would attribute sexuality to the "innocent babe"! What kind of lecherous villain was he who could "reduce" human behavior to sexual needs! As so often happens with the work of a creative genius, the very things for which Freud was attacked most vitriolically have proved to be among his most important contributions. As long as we remember, as Freud himself did, that sex is not the only human need, we find that his theses about sexuality immeasurably advance our understanding of human behavior.

But let us examine the proposition that the constancy of the pleasure principle shows us something about the constancy of human nature. It does so, again, only when we are thinking about human nature abstractly. When we get down to cases, it delivers less than it promises. Let us take the case of adult sexuality itself. We can say that both heterosexual and homosexual practices are obvious manifestations of sexual need. To say that the homosexual individual has the "same" need as the heterosexual, however, is to rob experience of its distinctions and deprive it of a good part of its meaning. Sexuality in the one case is different from the other just because its manifestations are different. Or take the case of homosexuality in our culture, with its stigma and furtiveness, as against homosexuality in a culture that openly accepts and perhaps dignifies it. The differing social attitudes make them as genuinely different as water containing typhus bacilli is different from water fit for drinking. The same considerations apply to cases of sublimation, the ability of a person to find expression for sexual need indirectly, through some kind of creative work. For the sublimation of a musician is not the same as that of a bridge builder, except abstractly, and the general conception gives us only partial understanding of the specific differences.

In all such cases, abstractions about human nature can be fruitful when they are seen in the context of a human nature that changes. They become strait jackets to our understanding when they are thought of as defining exclusively what human nature is and always has to be.

After taking this circuitous route, we can better see what Dewey means when he declares that human nature changes in accordance with the culture in which it is organized. When a culture stresses the belief that the virtues of an enemy can be drained from him by partaking of his flesh, human nature is cannibalistic. When a culture believes that the stranger is the same as the enemy, human nature is clannish. When a culture believes that there is a scarcity of available goods and that every man should take care of himself alone, human nature is rapacious; or if it believes that the answer lies in a co-operative attitude, then human nature is co-operative. When a culture stresses sexual prowess, man is dominated by the sexual motive; when it stresses unquestioning obedience, man is dominated by a sheeplike motive; when it stresses money, man is dominated by the pecuniary motive. Or if it puts emphasis on any two or three of these simultaneously, then these become the basic "drives" in human nature.

There is not a single human motive that is not a motivation of the culture itself. *Why* any one culture places a premium on certain motives as against others can be answered only by a careful study of the conditions of that culture's existence. This question is a branch of comparative ethnology, and it throws light on many hitherto dark chambers of human experience. *That* a culture makes such emphases, however, is why human nature is what it is found to be. The enlightening thing about it is that, the more detailed one makes these comparative studies, the more one is struck by the differences instead of the likenesses in human nature. When a culture prizes one set of motives above others, it is voicing its relative evaluation of all the motives possible in human behavior. And when a survey of various cultures leads us to arrange motives in an order of preference, we are voicing our relative evaluation, which means that we are making ethical judgments.

All this leaves us in a rather startling predicament, for we find that Dewey has brought us to the point of departing radically from traditional approaches to human nature and conduct. Traditionally, whatever the treatment of human motivation in its cultural manifestations, human nature was thought to be composed of some essential "drives" or "instincts." The problem of a scientific psychology was taken to be the problem of determining what these instincts actually are. Major quarrels raged over the truth or falsity of certain classifications, but they were quarrels within the family, and all the members of the family started with the same assumptions. They assumed, among other things, that they were engaged in meaningful quarrels. Then Dewey came along and asked us if these controversies are not actually as meaningless as many traditional battles in philosophy. He asked if, having made the wrong assumptions, we have not been putting the wrong questions.

The basic assumption of the tradition was that behavior had somehow to be "accounted for," and that instincts were the best answer to that need. Accordingly, the complex community life of ants and bees was thought to be evidence of a gregarious instinct. The procreative acts of lower animals were taken as evidence of a mating instinct. The ability of fish to swim, birds to fly, monkeys to climb, and horses to run were all regarded as instinctual. And by a simple transfer from the lower animals to human beings, it was "natural" to ask what were the instincts characterizing human nature.

Evidently it did not occur to these earlier thinkers that the theory of instincts answered nothing and only added another mystery. It answered nothing because in reality it was simply putting the original problem in other words: for example, talk about a gregarious instinct was just another way of saying that animals have social relations. When we say that fish swim, we have parially described what fish *are*, and there is something long-winded if not devious in saying that they do so instinctively. What is meant by a reference to instincts, of course, is that organisms behave in certain ways spontaneously, without being trained in those ways. But the folly of the explanation is patent when we look at it from another angle. The tendency of flowers to turn toward the sun can conveniently be summed up in the word "tropism," and that is meaningful discourse. If we then proceed to say that flowers turn toward the sun *because* of tropism, we are talking nonsense. What is so easily apparent in this case is more difficult to see in the case of instincts, but it is an identical situation. The identity is obscured by long habits of thought and speech. The instinct theory, aside from accounting for nothing, presents the added difficulty of giving us something more to be accounted for: namely, the meaning and origin of instincts themselves.

Essentially, the attribution of instincts to human beings is one phase of the habit of attributing "forces" to nature. In reporting an accident, we commonly say that windows miles away were shattered by the force of the explosion; or we account for a hurricane's destructiveness by referring to the force of the wind; or we speak of an airplane's defying the force of gravity. There was a time when physicists thought and wrote in these same terms, and that gave scientific "authority" to our common habit, which is probably rooted in primitive animism. Now the physicists have freed themselves from this naïve mysticism, and it is high time the rest of us did so. Windows are not shattered by the force of an explosion; they are shattered because they occupy a certain relation to the air blasts which are the explosion. There is no force behind a hurricane's destructiveness; air currents of a certain speed are destructive and are the hurricane. There is no force of gravity; gravitation is simply our collective term for describing what happens to bodies having a certain relation to each other. In other words "force," which was once thought of as having a status of its own, is now seen to be nothing but a metaphorical expression; and because of its metaphysical connotations, it is a dangerous metaphor. Exactly the same thing is true of "instincts" in human nature.

That all human beings have sexual needs, however they are expressed; that all human beings experience hunger, however it is satisfied; that all human beings require affection, however it is manifested—these propositions are not denied in a rejection of the instinct theory. What is denied is that sex, hunger, and affection exist apart from their means of expression. What is affirmed is that the "howevers," the means of expression, determine what our experiences of sex, hunger, and affection are. So with all experience.

But apart from the theoretical niceties, what difference is made by rejecting the theory that human nature never changes and accepting the theory that it does? What difference is made by rejecting the instinct theory and accepting the theory that human nature is a function of cultural organization? The answer is that the differences are revolutionary, however simply they may be stated. For the Deweyan position means that no limits can properly be assigned to the capacities of human beings. Consequently, "human nature" is not to be regarded as determining the contours of social organization. On the contrary, social organization is to be seen as largely determining what human nature is to be. In other words, every form of social organization is an expression of interests (by no means just economic interests). It expresses, consciously or unconsciously, explicitly or implicitly, the preponderant interests in producing certain kinds of human beings. Plato had a good deal of insight into this fact, which is why he insisted that the rules of the ideal republic would have to stress the doing of certain things while rigorously excluding certain others. His insight was overweighted, however, and in the end sunk by the metaphysical structure which, according to one interpretation, he built and which the tradition inherited and developed. Dewey, dynamiting the superstructure, has helped us to see the foundations for what they are. He has gone further. He has helped us to see how the foundations are laid, leaving it to us to dig them out, if we so choose, in order to lay other foundations better suited to the structure we might like to erect.

For all the headaches and heartaches of the contemporary world, therefore, we see that we are in a commanding position with respect to the future. Better than any age in the history of mankind, we are able to see the wonderful malleability, the infinite plasticity, of human nature. From the viewpoint of easy intellectual classification, this has its difficulties, which is one reason why so many traditionalists resist Dewey's whole approach to the matter. We have a much simpler intellectual problem if we can say that human nature is $A$, $B$, $C$, and $D$, and then spell out various ways in which these elements can be combined—it is simpler to do this than to say that human nature is a complicated $X$, with the $X$ varying in subtle ways according to changes in social conditions. But while, from this point of view, our difficulties are increased, from another point of view our problems are simplified. For instead of having to resign ourselves to human nature's being what it is, and making the best of it, we see that its plasticity makes some of our highest ambitions practical possibilities. No longer can the "realists" dismiss the longings for a good and peaceful world as utopian fantasies, or will-o'-the-wisps. In doing so, they convict themselves: of absolutism, of prejudice, of narrow vested or self-interests which they attempt to cloak in the cover of "fact." We can see, rather, that the clarification of the interests involved in every social struggle is one step in the clarification of the desired goals of mankind. And we can see, further, that the clarification of the goals, dependent as it is on the use of intelligence, in turn opens the way for the free use of intelligence in the pursuit of them. If this sounds like circularity of reasoning, it is not of the vicious kind. It is one expression of that inseparable interplay between means and ends which characterizes the life process, in which intelligence is, because it has to be, man's chief reliance.

All this that Dewey has helped us to see about human nature and its possibilities would have been impossible without James's earlier work in the psychology of habit. But Dewey has pushed us further, enabling us better to understand that although habit is individual in function, it is largely social in origin. Ordinarily, we think of habits in intensely personal ways, as being peculiarly "ours." *We* smoke or drink or swear too much, fritter away our time on trivial matters, stay up too late at night—and the "we" in question is always oneself. More often than not, evidently when we think of habits we think of the "bad" ones, and this probably has its origin in our early childhood, when parents and other adults were disciplining us. Thus, if we bit our fingernails, we may well have been encouraged to break the habit, or scolded or punished in the effort to force us to do so. This would be true of many other things that were deemed personally undesirable or socially offensive. Since these were the habits to which our attention was called, it is obvious why "habit" spontaneously connotes "bad" for so many of us. The habits that were encouraged—brushing our teeth and keeping ourselves clean, eating "properly" at the table, playing co-operatively with other children—ordinarily no reference was made to these as being habits.

James drove home for us the indispensable role played by "good" habits in everyday life—that if we did not dress and eat and do much of our routine work by habit, without thinking, it would be literally impossible for us to carry on the business of living. That is why, in the interest of promoting the expression of our better possibilities, he urged that we act on a good intention whenever we have it, with the thought that such action might then become habitual with us. His emphasis on the importance of our acting on such intentions was a consequence of his grounding habit physiologically, in our bodily structures. He thus pioneered, in ways that have had enormous implications, in co-ordinating the relations of body and mind, which has had one flowering in the contemporary concern with psychosomatic medicine.

It was this that provided the basis for Dewey's thinking about human nature and, as we have seen, enabled him to overcome the dualism between mind and body. Traditionally, men thought of bodies as "having" minds or of minds inhabiting bodies; as, for some theologians, the soul is thought to enter the body, either at the time of conception or some subsequent date. For Dewey, this is so false a picture that he has searched, not too successfully, for some other way of speaking about it. He has had to resort to the use of a hyphen to make clear that human beings are not bodies and minds but are body-minds. Again, as in the case of "warranted assertibility" in place of "truth," "body-mind" is not too happy an expression. But the search for a substitute is not likely to yield any better results, and it has the virtue of making somewhat clearer what is meant. When the dualistic tradition is sometime liquidated, and the sciences of human behavior have resolved some of our present problems, we shall be able to use such simple expressions as "human beings" and "persons" without confusion. The basic point involved is so important, however, that it is worth repetition. Dewey does not think of a person as having a body and a mind; the person *is* body-mind.

Now James, coupling his genius for insight with an intense concern for individuality, treated the psychology of habit in primarily individual terms. And indeed, as we know, whatever social philosophy we may hold, it is never "society" that functions, but always the individuals who compose it. Just so are habits expressed individually, to such an extent that we are justified in saying that our peculiarly individual clusters of habits largely define our individuality. But while habits are thus individual in expression, they are social in origin, and we cannot really understand them without also understanding this. It is here that Dewey has made so important a contribution to our understanding, a contribution inseparable from his philosophy of education.

We have fallen into the unfortunate custom of speaking of individual psychology and social psychology. Although essentially we have had in mind a distinction between different fields of research, it has sometimes led people to believe that there is "an" individual as distinct from "a" social psychology. Nothing could be more misleading. And when it helps to perpetuate the dualism between individual and society, it is disastrous. When Dewey is thought of as contributing to social psychology, therefore, we have to keep in mind that he is giving us additional insight into individual behavior. At the same time, such insight is indispensable to the reconstruction of our social institutions.

What do we mean, then, by saying that habits are social in origin? On reflection, it is a commonplace, and there are countless illustrations of it. On arising in the morning, we get up out of beds which, for all their variation of design, are socially standardized. We brush our teeth with our own toothbrushes in our own ways, but society (through our parents and teachers) has educated us to do so, our brushes are almost identical with other people's, and even the best ways of brushing are the fruits of dental research passed on to us by dentists or hygienists. We bathe or shower because society has taught us the values of cleanliness, and we breakfast on foods that are much the same as those of our next-door neighbors. If we live in a city, most of us go to work in public means of conveyance, and one woman does her housework with the same kind of equipment as do most others. If we are lawyers, we practice the law of our society; if we are doctors, we practice the medicine of our times; if we are clerks, we follow accepted trade practices and use standardized merchandise, standardized salesbooks, standardized cash registers; if we are bookkeepers we observe "accepted" methods of keeping books; if we are investment bankers, we watch the same movements of the same stock and bond markets and respond in much the same ways as do other bankers. And so on, up and down the line of our daily activities, with respect to most of the basic habits that are individually ours.

All this, as we have noted, is commonplace. But Dewey, in conjunction with George Herbert Mead and a handful of others, has brought us to the point where we can see some of the deeper implications of these facts. On the whole, we have been quite ready to accept it as obvious (at least, after it is pointed out to us) that our "selves" are expressed in social patterns, social institutions, or, if we so put it, social habits. What we have not so readily seen is that our very "selves" are created in the process; that we do not so much "express" habits as we are formed by them or, to put it more accurately, that in large measure we *are* our habits; and that, consequently, not merely our habits, but ourselves, are largely social in origin.

This is a simple insight to state, but a hard one to grasp. For much of everything in our upbringing, and our accustomed ways of thinking about ourselves in relation to others, is against it. Ordinarily, we give no thought to ourselves at all. We go about our business, concerned with only those aspects of ourselves as may present problems. Aside from periodic routine visits, for example, we go to the dentist only if we have a toothache, which obliges us to think about that part of ourselves and do something about it. We go to a doctor when we are ill or have an accident, and most of the time, unless we are hypochondriacs, we do not think about our health. As a rule, we accept the fact that we look the way we do, until some situation arises or someone makes some remarks that turn our special attention to our appearance. In these, and multitudes of other ways, we take ourselves for granted—and from this point of view, it is just as well that we do so.

Sometimes, however, when we are in a reflective mood not occasioned by any specific problem, we may speculate about ourselves and the world in which we live. At such times, customarily, we are inclined to think of ourselves as independent entities "having" relations with other people and the things of the world. In other words, when we think about ourselves, more frequently than not we take our egos or personalities as "givens," and we may then go on to ponder about how the outer world affects us and we affect it. The age-long theological tradition of self-existent souls is probably one reason for this; the widespread emotional need to see oneself, one's ego, as indestructible, as enduring indefinitely or eternally, is another. However that may be, we contrapose the ego and the other, the self and society, and we are faced with the resultant problem of relating if not reconciling them intelligibly. When we approach matters in this way, we have the tendency to think that we become aware of other people and other things in distinction from ourselves: that is, it is as if we said that here we are, and there is something that is not here in us, and that is why we know it is something different from us, why it is an "other." This doubtless has a good deal to do with our inclination to regard habits as "expressing" our individuality.

One upshot of the social approach to human behavior is to reverse this picture. In the light of it, we perceive that the very recognition of ourselves may be dependent upon our prior recognition that others exist. It may well be true, for example, that the infant first becomes aware of the self when it recognizes that the mother, the father, the crib are somehow "others"; that everything is not wish and immediate fulfillment, but that there are things independent of wish that may frustrate it; that there are, in distinction from these things, others that are just wish and immediate fulfillment, such as thumb sucking; and that those things that are not immediate wish fulfillment define the boundaries and lead to the discovery of the self. There seems to be no way of verifying this hypothesis, as there is no clear way of refuting it. Whether it is literally true or not, however, it provides us with a richly suggestive insight into the nature of the self. For it enables us better to see the creative process involved, with this as an early stage in the creation of ourselves. And, even more important, it enables us to perceive how central a role is played by other people, by society, in the origins and development of personality.

The critical importance of the earliest period of one's life, the years of one's "forgotten childhood," has become familiar to us through the work of the psychoanalysts. We have learned that it is then that the basic personality patterns are shaped and set. These patterns are of central importance just because, being so much what we are and coloring everything we do, we are not aware of them. They are our unconscious attitudes and responses to people, things, and situations. Obviously, we cannot deal with anything intelligently until we do become aware of it. That is why psychoanalysis, having devised successful techniques for bringing such unconscious attitudes to our awareness, is so often helpful in resolving personality problems.

Psychoanalysis has brought with it a theoretical framework,

however, that threatens its major contributions to psychology if it is not distinguished from them. The jargon of the professionals has gradually become part of our common speech, and most of us are not only acquainted with such terms as "ego," "id," and "superego," but know that they are roughly equivalent, respectively, to conscious behavior, unconscious behavior, and conscientious behavior. If that were all there were to it, there would be no problem. But it is not all. For most professionals of an orthodox Freudian persuasian, and many laymen, do not use these terms in this way. They speak rather of *the* ego, *the* id, *the* superego, and instead of our being confronted with questions of the relation of unconscious to conscious activities, we are presented with *the* Unconscious, a metaphysical bugaboo spawned by nineteenth-century German philosophers. When unconscious activities are thus "thingified," when they are converted into an independent entity and then contrasted with the other two entities, *the* conscious self and *the* conscience, the realities of human behavior are falsified. Furthermore, new problems are created: how the parts of such a self are related to each other (some psychoanalysts even draw pictures of this for us!), how this three-part self is related to other selves, and how it is related to the rest of nature. Psychoanalysis, as psychological insight and science, has no business with these problems. They are unnecessary baggage, a deadweight which it carries at the expense of its strength and vitality.

If, instead of talking about "the Unconscious," we think of unconscious behavior, we can see the fruitful relation that is possible between the insights of Freud and his successors on the one hand and those of James and Dewey on the other. For what is "habit" but a collective term for the things we do unthinkingly, unconsciously? As small children, we quickly learn the things that please and displease our parents and others in our intimate world. These things need not be expressed verbally, and are often more influential when they are not; indeed, sometimes they cannot be, for they are expressions of the parents' unconscious attitudes. If a small child constantly plies his parents with questions about himself and the world he lives in, and is accustomed to straight-

forward answers, and then finds his questions about sex turned
aside with parental embarrassment, the embarrassment is what
registers and helps to shape the child's unconscious attitudes about
sex. These childhood experiences of what elicits parental pleasure
and displeasure, clustering into habitual attitudes and activities,
are the nerve centers of our emotional lives. If, with the psychoanalysts, we sum them up in the expression "the unconscious"
(without the capital "U"), we should be mindful that they do not
constitute some separate region in the psyche, that they are rather
the permeating context in which our conscious lives are lived.
In other words, "the unconscious" thus used is seen to be synony-
mous with our habitual attitudes and activities. When we think
of the matter in this way, James helps us to understand the biological and Dewey the social basis of "the unconscious," as Freud
gives us masterly perceptions of some of the internal, private implications of their work.

Having added this much thickness to our insight, let us return to the field of Dewey's special contributions, the social roots
of individual habits. It is true that our attitudes about sex, for
example, are in large measure shaped by our childhood relations
to our parents, and by what their attitudes are. If we pursued this
line of thought rigidly, we should have to point out that their attitudes, in turn, were shaped by their childhood relations to their
parents, and so on backward in indefinite regression. We would
wind up with the preposterous, not to say nonsensical, conclusion
that when we speak of parental influence on children, we are in
the last analysis talking about the influence of one childhood on
another, the finally determining childhood being that of the first
human beings. To put it differently, we would emerge as Freud
does with a secular version of original sin.

Fortunately, the facts of life prevent us from being reduced
to this ridiculous position. Important as are the experiences of
our earliest years, experiences throughout life are always coming
in on us to shape and reshape our attitudes and habits. But what is
the nature of such experience, from the viewpoint of our present
discussion? It is both private and public. Whatever the childhood

foundations of our sexual attitudes, and however private and in-duplicable they may be, our lives are lived in a society that has collective attitudes about sexual relations—or at least it purports to have them. The sociologists call these part of the *mores,* and some of them become institutionalized in our laws dealing with sexual relations. Now, Peirce once remarked that scientific laws are nothing but the habits of nature. In a different but related sense, we can say that the laws of a state or nation are among the habits of that society, statements of the customary or prevailingly desired ways of dealing with problems of human relations. In practice, of course, our sex attitudes are conditioned less by the legal codes than by the *mores* of the particular social group with which we feel primarily identified. But one way or another, the social attitudes become part and parcel of our private attitudes, whatever individual twists we may give them. And it is these com-plexly formed attitudes, with their wide social reaches, and not something preserved in pristine purity from our own childhood, that we bring to bear as parents on our children. In other words, these habitual attitudes have a social origin not merely in the sense that they are shaped by other members of our families, but in the far more significant sense that the attitudes of our society are integral parts of ourselves. Dewey somewhere remarks that through our habits we in-habit the world. Reversing the coin in the light of what we have just been saying, we can observe that with the passage of time we do not simply acquire information about the society of which we are part, but that our society literally in-forms us.

Consider, now, some of the practical implications of this view of human nature. If what we are as individuals is largely a matter of our unconscious attitudes and motivations, if "the unconscious" is largely commensurate with our habits, and if our habits are largely social in origin, then the individual and society are inseparable. We may separate them for purposes of special analysis and research, but if we continue to view them as separate in the flow of experience, our vision is distorted. We may then emphasize the party or society or the state to the detriment of

the individual, as is characteristic of totalitarian movements. Or
we may stress the individual at the expense of social considerations, as is characteristic of "rugged individualism." Either way,
we have lost track of the arteries that stem from the heart of the
relationship. This is not to deny that the richest significance of
societies lies in the individuals they produce. It does. It is rather
to affirm that the existing institutions of society—language, education, morality, law, economy, religion—are integral parts of
the individuals produced. Concern with social institutions, therefore, is essential to any realistic concern with the enrichment of
individuality, with raising the level of individual performance.
That is why, as we shall see in a moment, the issues of social
reconstruction have loomed so large in Dewey's mind.

It is also the point of departure for his philosophy of education. When Dewey left the University of Michigan in 1894, to
become chairman of the department of philosophy at the newly
formed University of Chicago, he was already on the way to
working out the views that are now so intimately associated with
his name. Part of the lure of the new post was the opportunity for
establishing, under his direction, an experimental school for children, in which he might test some of his educational theories.
That school was to become one of the most celebrated experiments in the history of education, and through it and the writings
that stemmed from his work with it, Dewey was to leave a timeless imprint on our school systems, on our views of the ways in
which education should be carried on, and on the very meaning
of education. That his imprint is timeless cannot be taken to
mean, however, that his theories have overcome all opposition.
This is so far from being the case that the chief struggle in the
contemporary educational world is to keep them from being
pushed aside by new versions of traditional views which, despite
the disclaimers of their proponents, are conservative and sometimes reactionary in their methods and aims. Dewey is, above all
else, the philosopher of democracy. If democracy is evolutionary
rather than revolutionary in its methods, then education, as hosts
of people since Jefferson's time have realized, is the key to the

process. Democracy and education go hand in hand, and Dewey was not at all exaggerating when he wrote many years ago, after he had moved on to Columbia University and become a distinguished professor there, that his educational theories are a handle to his whole philosophy.

Education is, after all, inseparable from our theories of human nature. To those who assume that human nature is fixed and unchanging, it follows that society has to be organized along certain lines in order to meet the actualities of what human beings are. It follows, further, that the function of a basic education is so to raise children and adolescents that they will adequately find their individual places in society. In addition, if human nature is what it is, once and for all, then the methods by which individuals learn anything can be carefully observed and, once they are clearly seen, they can be standardized as educational procedure. Pedagogues will be aware, of course, that learning is relative to the things to be learned. And the things to be learned will be regarded as those which, out of the accumulated experience of the human race, have proved essential to survival and beneficial to carrying on the work of the world. The key to education for such people, accordingly, is "training" and "disciplining" the mind and person, so that the little savages that children are (repeating, in their lifetimes, the evolutionary stages of humanity) may be fashioned into the civilized adults that contemporary society demands.

Unfortunately, the "culture," which designates what anthropologists mean by the total organizational complex of a society, is subdivided into the Culture of a cultured gentleman on the one hand and the ways of making a living on the other. The former, Culture, is the essence of the aristocratic tradition, embracing the humanities and the arts. Logic and mathematics, Greek and Latin, rhetoric and theology or metaphysics—these are the studies through which the intractable child is taught to become the acceptable gentleman. They are to be taught by repetition and imitation, if not by rote, and the educational process becomes, in its way, as much a ritual as any ecclesiastical organization could wish. Unfortunately, again, the native abilities of many children are so "deficient" that they cannot participate in this learning process. By definition, therefore, they cannot genuinely share in the Culture that distinguishes Education. Nevertheless, they, too, have lives to be lived. What is to happen to them? The only education for which they are fitted is not properly education at all. That is, it is not a matter of training their minds for the "higher things" of life, but training their hands to do the physical work that has to be done. Put differently, they are fit primarily for vocational education, which is so different in aim and methods as to be a universe apart from liberal education. In a nutshell, "education" is of two different kinds: liberal, for those who will be the cultured leaders of society, and vocational, for those who will support them by the sweat of their labor.

This has been the dominant tradition in Western education, however it has been overlarded and disguised. And its revival by Robert M. Hutchins and other leaders of "education for freedom" is one of the superb ironies of a democratic society. One way or another, however, despite the aims of democracy, the fixed view of human nature has fathered educational methods that perpetuate the aristocratic tradition.

What follows educationally from Dewey's opposing view that human nature is not fixed, but is itself one of the changing, growing aspects of experience? In broad terms, as we have noted, it means that no limits can be set to the possibilities possessed by human beings. At the same time, if democracy as a way of life means anything at all, it means a profound faith in these very possibilities. The key problem of democratic education, accordingly, is to devise methods that will stimulate the development of individual possibilities, whatever they are, and regardless of traditionally accepted views of "learning." When this problem is seen in the context of the psychology of habit, and we remember that habit is both physiological and social in its origins, revolutionary implications for education are the consequence. It was these implications that Dewey saw and began to put to work over half a century ago in his experimental school. They were to become the core of what was later to be known as "progressive" education.

The slogan of the new movement was universally echoed, though frequently misunderstood. The slogan was that we "learn by doing." Nothing could better state the educational consequences of the James-Dewey psychology of habit. It is not so much what we read or hear or say that affects and shapes what we are, but how our bodily responses and our attitudes are conditioned by our activities, by our interactions with people and things. Education, therefore, is not to be viewed passively, as the means by which already established knowledge is poured into the receptacles that are children. On the contrary, education is first and foremost a matter of active participation. Not only that: no outsider can determine what are an individual's possibilities by looking at him or casually observing him in the process of rote learning, nor can the individual himself know what they are until he discovers them. The observation that life is a process of trial and error is especially relevant in the case of children. "Doing," it is evident, has a twofold importance. First, it is the method by which we carry on significant learning, learning that is so incorporated into our persons as to be an essential part of what we are. Second, it is the method by which we discover what we are. The Deweyan revolution in education, we see, has already carried us a long way. For instead of regarding education as the rote learning of what is already known, it takes the educational process as primarily a matter of discovering our possibilities and of devising methods that will help us both to discover and develop them.

Here we come face to face with another major aspect of this revolution. For what has been the traditional view of education? Down at the bottom, it was to regard children as little adults. However relevant or irrelevant certain things might be to childhood experience, they were to be taught as essential parts of the equipment of adults. Children themselves might not be able to see the importance of these things and might even rebel against them, but there was no harm in that. Vanquished rebellion itself was thought to be good for the discipline of their unruly spirits, and it was the responsibility of adults to teach them what sometime they would have to know, no matter what they thought of it. Who knows better than adults what adult life means, and childhood is a preparation for adult life. Here a hidden metaphysics enters, and shows again the practical bearing of some of our most abstract speculations. When childhood is thought of as basically a preparation for adult life, it is part of a longer view: that life itself is essentially preparation for a hereafter. But assume, instead, that life is not a preparation, that it is rather whatever it appears to be and is experienced as being. Assume that childhood, in the same terms, is not a preparation for a later stage, but is what it is and is to be lived on its own account. It follows that if the meanings of life are to be found in the fullest and richest experiences, the concern of education should be to help children to the richest experiences possible for them. This is where Dewey took his stand, on the proposition that children are not little adults but are people in their own right and in their own ways.

The consequences are of tremendous import, both for education and democracy. There can be no hard-and-fast distinctions between Culture and work, between liberal and vocational education. Whatever one's possibilities and distinctive abilities, his education should be liberating, in the sense of freeing and developing his unique qualities through creative effort. The efforts themselves, based as they should be on one's deepest interests, are the means of both training and discipline. For whatever the opposing theories, experience points to the fact that we are really trained and disciplined as persons by the conditions of what we are trying to do. A person becomes a trained public speaker through practice in public speaking, and not through merely thinking about the matter. A person becomes a trained psychoanalyst by practicing analysis, not by speculating about it. To be sure, there must be adequate guidance in these and in all other fields of endeavor, but the guidance alone can never make an adequate practitioner. That is achieved, rather, through the discovery of our own powers in the process itself. We would do well to ponder the implication of our common speech habits, which lead us to speak of a lawyer as one who practices law, of a doctor as one who practices medicine.

The same thing holds of discipline. We can be forced to behave in certain ways, through the exercise of authority and the threat of punishment. This is the premise of much social organization, as it is of much religion. But again, this is a valid attitude only if we view human beings as potential barbarians who have to be molded into acceptable patterns, passive instruments in the hands of a superior wisdom. If, instead of this, we think of personality as something to be achieved, of our very selves as in the process of creation, then discipline takes on an altogether different meaning. Then it becomes evident that, just as a sprinter can never hope to break the record for the hundred-yard dash if he does not discipline himself to a rigid regimen of physical training, so whatever we genuinely hope to achieve and become sets its own requirements on us. It is this inner discipline, relative to the ends we have in view, which is the democratic counter to the discipline of authority.

These general considerations have vast consequences for education. Primarily, and always in intention if not in practice, teachers animated by the Deweyan philosophy see learning as dynamically related to a child's developing interests. That is, the old ritualistic approach is discarded: the attitude that at a certain age, regardless of other considerations, a child should be taught the alphabet, spelling, reading, writing, the multiplication tables, and so on. Instead of this mechanical movement through the stages of a fixed curriculum, instead of this dry-as-dust drilling of children in routine procedures thought to train their memories and their minds, education is seen as a series of exciting undertakings, experiments, projects. The special subjects are related to the child's discovery of himself and his world. If he is interested in playing store, for example, he finds that there are things he must know in order to carry on his play: how to count, to add, to multiply, to read and write. These things, he finds, are essential to the transactions that give meaning to his play, and he is eager to learn them.

At the same time, in spite of the claims of the tradition, the new educational philosophy in practice shows greater respect for individuality, a greater sensitivity to the differences among individuals. One child of six may be ready to read, another may not be; one may be quick to grasp arithmetic, another completely baffled by it; one may be lightninglike in his verbal responses while poorly co-ordinated physically, another may be just the reverse. Granted these and hosts of other differences, coupled with a genuine respect for individuality, the problem of education is not to make all children alike or try to mold them to conform to some ideal model of child development. But implicitly, traditional education has done just this, making invidious distinctions among children in the light of its fixed standards. This is the root of the mechanical system of grading pupils on report cards, setting up false criteria of performance for them and their parents, and giving edge to a sense of competition that is often destructive. The child who is verbally slow, and therefore seemingly stupid in regular classroom work, may be gifted manually and easily the leader of his group in shopwork—but the educational tradition, reflecting the class distinctions of the larger society, has seen him as fit only for vocational training, and he may carry the brand-mark of inferiority around with him for a lifetime.

Instead of this traditional approach, which has had harmful effects on numberless individuals, the project method of the new educational philosophy is aimed at eliciting the contributions each individual is able to make to a common effort. If a group of children wish to set up and operate a model store, different abilities are not only desirable but necessary to the project. One child may have organizational ability and administer the undertaking, another do the necessary shopwork for the equipment, a third the posters for the promotion of merchandise, a fourth the actual merchandising, a fifth the bookkeeping. The child's feeling of group loyalty and his sense of responsibility for the success of the project stimulate him to the best contribution he can make along the line of his own, distinctive abilities. They also force him to see his place and his specific functions in the light of the group effort. The understanding and attitudes which are fashioned in the process are far more fruitful in the long run than the competitive yardsticks that measure children against each other and by some ideal standard. The way is opened, rather, to the discovery of oneself and to learning something of the hard discipline imposed by a desired goal.

Central as this is, Dewey's approach to schooling does not stop with it. In the days of the little red schoolhouse, for all the educational deficiencies, there was one great advantage too often ignored by earlier theorizers. The school was in the community. When they were not in school, the children worked in the fields with adults. In other words, they were in the common life and the common life was in them. In rural communities even today, despite the mechanization and complication of existence, children experience a good deal of this. But with the urbanization of life, the school became an isolated community of its own, having only a tenuous relation to the wider community, almost, indeed, superimposed upon it. It is no wonder that a good deal of education seemed irrelevant to ordinary experience, that even the "problems" presented to children as challenges for the training of their minds were artificial. The whole atmosphere was permeated with the artificiality of an old-fashioned language textbook, in which one would be taught to say, in French or Spanish or German or whatever, "The pen is on the table near the blackboard"—which is all right in its way, except that one seldom has any occasion to say it! Nothing better illustrates the basic shift in educational methods than the new, conversational approach to a foreign tongue, through which one learns to speak what he has need to say in order to carry on the business of life, in much the same way as a child learns his native language.

Now if the problem of education is the development of an individual's possibilities, and if those possibilities are not "academic" but are inseparable from the life he lives outside of school, then there ought to be a dynamic relation between the school and the wider community. This is the background consideration in the pedagogical emphasis in recent years on field trips—to factories, shipyards, mines, business offices, food markets—in an attempt to implement the idea that schooling is not something carried on inside school buildings alone, but involves firsthand acquaintance with basic features of the world we live in. Despite the years in which the Deweyan philosophy of education has had the chance to work its way, however, we are still only at the threshold of the problem, with faint glimmerings of what it means to make the larger community part of the school, the school an integral part of the community.

We can see, then, that while "learning by doing" is a simple slogan, easily parroted, it is not an easy thing to put to work in the life of education. It is manifestly an infinitely harder task than traditional schooling. It requires of teachers a patience, an insight, a training, a flexibility, and above all a love of children that surpasses anything previously expected of them. It requires of school administrations a realization that children do not exist in order to be ground through the mills of a formalized system, but that the system exists in order to educate children in terms of their best possibilities, whatever they are. It requires of parents the knowledge that they have to stop projecting their own ego needs onto their children, attempting to satisfy their competitive drives through the children's competitive performances; and it requires of them, too, a willingness to see that the home atmosphere and attitudes have as much to do with schooling as anything that happens in the school. Finally, it requires of the community at large, the taxpayers, a day-to-day sense of its responsibilities to the oncoming generations and to the future of democracy, a readiness to pay in hard cash for the education it says is central to our way of life.

Yes, it is easy to say that we learn by doing, but the principle cuts two ways, as Dewey himself has pointed out. We can learn the wrong things by putting the wrong ideas to work and doing the wrong things. To learn the fruitful, constructive things we need to learn means putting the right ideas to work in the right ways. And that requires nothing less than the hard and earnest use of intelligence in the planning of experiences through which it will be good to learn.

Yet in the last analysis, schooling is only one part of education, and by no means the most important part. We are educated by our total culture, by the institutions that comprise it. We are educated by the language we speak and in which we think, by our family life, by our ways of earning a living, by our political and social activities, by our recreational life, by the prevailing morality. These culture patterns have far more to do with what we are than anything that happens in the schools. We are forced to the realization that when we talk about relying on education as the method of democracy, we are talking about reconstructing our social institutions. This reconstruction Dewey regards as a necessity if we are to free the possibilities in human nature.

# CHAPTER FOUR

# DEMOCRACY AS A WAY OF LIFE

DEMOCRACY is a faith in the possibilities of human nature. But when we have said this much, what have we really said?

In our time, the possibilities for evil are only too apparent on all sides. This is what accounts for the resurgence of religious orthodoxy. It is also what accounts for authoritarianism, whether in religion or economics, in social organization or politics. Having seen the evil fruits of some of man's possibilities, the authoritarian is one who has faith in human nature only as it is subject to his guidance and dictation.

A "benevolent" dictator may sometimes graciously avow that he is only helping people to the point where they can live good lives in their own ways instead of in his. All his actions, nevertheless, are based on the belief that the masses of men would brutishly betray their own best possibilities were it not for his tutelage and control. The fly in the ointment, of course, is that he sets himself up as absolute judge of what people's "best" possibilities really are. What is he to say, then, to those who claim that every man knows best where the shoe pinches on his own foot? He will say nothing. He will simply shut them up. This is the way of every dictatorship, every absolutism, every inquisition, every police state—call it what you will. And the way is always justified as being some holy mission, however revealed and however described. For the mission is to save men, in spite of themselves, from the evil that is in them. Only one who "knows" can do that.

Yet democracy *is* faith in man's possibilities. It is not politics alone, for if it were and man were essentially evil, government would continuously degenerate. It is not economics alone, for if it were and man were essentially evil, we would before now have become a nation of slaves. It is not social alone, for if it were and man were essentially evil, we would be driven by an iron aristocracy. No, democracy is neither a political nor an economic nor a social concern taken separately. Nor is it just all of them taken together. It is rather, as Dewey has said, a moral ideal, a statement of the relations that *should* prevail among human beings. It is the hypothesis, if not the belief, that if man creates the proper institutions, then his better possibilities will actualize themselves.

From this point of view, all of human history, to say nothing of pre-history, has been a prelude. As Emerson once observed, we stand but at the cockcrow of civilization. Over the ages, what has been the burden of experience for the masses of men? Nothing but endless, back-breaking labor to wrest subsistence from a niggardly nature. The person of culture was able to cultivate the arts which made him so only because he had reached the position where he could squeeze his living out of other people's sweat. Now modern science, technology, and industry have changed all that, even though most of us continue to think about life in the same hoary old terms. Now man, instead of working himself to death for a living that is never adequate, finds nature burgeoning with riches past anything he had ever dreamed. Now experience, instead of a narrow, one-way street, can be for everyone a system of interlacing highways reaching over the most distant hills, and beyond that, and still beyond.

There are many ways of getting at the main emphasis of Dewey's work. One of the most fruitful is to see it as a continuous, consistent effort to provide a coherent and valid statement of the democratic potentials in modern experience. His ceaseless attacks upon dualisms of every kind, and especially upon those between theory and practice, knowledge and opinion, ends and means, can properly be regarded as attacks upon an aristocratic, leisure-class condescension toward the world of the masses of men.

We have seen that scientific method is central to Dewey's thinking. We have also seen that while scientists themselves are technical specialists in one field or another, their ways of attaining knowledge do not differ in kind from the ways in which the rest of us generally get to know anything in our daily lives. When we say that scientific method brings democracy to the knowledge-process, we mean that there are no final "truths" laid down once and for all by some authority which everybody has to accept. We mean, instead, that every proposition is open to doubt and subsequent testing by anyone competent to inquire into it.

What does this have to do with the enrichment and democratization of experience? Does it mean that everyone ought to become a scientist? Not at all. It means something far broader and deeper than this. It means that mankind will not gain the human riches that scientific method makes available to us until we rid ourselves of dogmas, of all the metaphysical, theological, political, social, economic, and other absolutes that have blinded us for centuries. It means that we have literally to see ourselves and the world differently. For what we see is not simply a matter of the way in which different light rays affect our eyes and brains. We see things in the light of accumulated experience, our own and others', the fund of meanings we bring to each and every perception. It is this fund of meanings that comprises our common sense. And the necessity of modern man is to reconstruct it, to create a new common sense.

On the face of it, this is a preposterous proposal. Common sense is both common (that is, generally held) and sense (that is, presumably valid) just because it is grounded in so much experience and continuously tested by it. So, for example, when we say that an acquaintance of ours doesn't know enough to come in out of the rain, we mean that he is not very bright, that he lacks judgment or common sense. Or when we say that another friend has a good deal of common sense, we mean that if he is confronted with a problem he will show sound judgment in dealing with it.

In other words, whenever we judge that a given individual does or does not have common sense, we are reaching an important practical conclusion. Common sense is our secure medium of exchange in carrying on commerce with other people and the world we live in.

A "secure" medium of exchange, we say. In this period of world-wide inflation, however, we have learned that any such medium, even the soundest, is only relatively secure. To be sure, a dollar bill, as a piece of paper, still looks the same as it did before World War II. But because it will only buy about half as much, it means something quite different; for example, it may mean four gallons of gasoline instead of eight. On the other hand, there are more dollar bills, and most of us get more of them more easily than we did ten years ago; so that a dollar may mean working a half hour instead of an hour. Both in terms of what it will buy and what we have to do to get it, therefore, a dollar is not only worth less, but we value it less. To put the matter differently, there are constantly shifting meanings within any given medium of exchange. Just so, though perhaps not so obviously, there are constantly shifting meanings within any system of common sense.

Now we know that if the process of inflation gets out of hand, as it did in Germany after World War I, the medium of exchange becomes meaningless. That is, the printing presses turn out billions of bills that are not only worth less and less, but finally become worthless. In that event, there has to be a return to "reality." A nation has to go back to the facts of its economic life, try to determine what those facts mean in terms of the living standards of its population, and set up a new monetary system based on that determination.

Nothing so dramatically drastic as this can happen with respect to common sense. Yet there come times in human development when the accumulated fund of meanings which is common sense becomes relatively worthless in dealing with the world. This is what happened at the time of the rise of Christianity, when a new religion came to give new meaning to a world that had lost its nerve. It took centuries for that new religion to broaden into a generally accepted attitude, a climate of opinion. It happened again with the rise of modern science a few centuries ago, when it became evident to competent inquirers that the old theological explanations were inadequate for carrying on the business of life. The new meanings that have come with it have slowly but surely gained wider acceptance, but they are far from having become a climate of opinion. This is what causes our crisis of common sense. For we live in a world largely made by the new techniques and technologies, but we see it through the eyes of the old meanings.

If we agree with Dewey that the primary concern of philosophy is to help point directions for making life more meaningful, we see that we have now moved away from the paper work and the laboratory and have reached the philosopher's proving ground. Will our theories, put to the crucial test, result in a successful experiment? Or will they, quite literally, blow up in our faces? We can imagine the anxiety, the trepidation, with which some of the world's most distinguished scientists gathered in the deserts of New Mexico for the critical test of the atom bomb. How much greater must be our anxiety as we test these broader propositions, for on the outcome depends the future of humanity. And right here is the difficulty. For no given tract of land, but the whole world, is our proving ground. No handful of nuclear explosive, but the social and political institutions of mankind, is our material. No one experiment, but the interplay of peoples for a half century or more, is our crucial test. Meanwhile, we have still to see the problem.

The problem is to reconstruct our institutions so that they express, not the common sense we have inherited from the ancient world and the middle ages, but the kind of knowledge with which we operate our machines. This is a tricky problem, as is evident as soon as we tackle any phase of it. Take the matter of language alone. Language is a tool of communication, devised for the purpose of helping one person know what another person means. It is effective if the words used are clear in what they refer to, and if people agree about that reference. If a child is at the table and asks, "May I have some jelly and a piece of bread?", the meaning is clear. It is clear, that is, if there is only one kind of jelly and one kind of bread on the table. If there are more than one of either or both, then he will have to be more specific in order to communicate with the others sitting with him. By being more specific, however, he can still communicate clearly. Think back to our illustration of various ways in which the word "knowledge" is used, on the other hand, and see the morass of confusion in which we can get ourselves. Or take the word "religion." In any specifiable sense, it means something quite different to a Roman Catholic, a Protestant, a Jew, a fundamentalist, a modernist, a theosophist, an agnostic, an atheist, or a comparative ethnologist. If we then go on to picture a representative of each of these positions gathered in the same room to discuss religion, we get the difficulties of communication in a nutshell. Or let us imagine a lover of Liszt and Chopin, hearing for the first time a work of Schoenberg and irately demanding, "Do you call that music!" Or a devotee of academic art first seeing an exhibition of abstract painting and caustically remarking, "You may say that's art, but my six-year-old son can make doodles that look better than that!"

Now general words such as "knowledge," "religion," and "art" are indispensable to communication. But they successfully serve a purpose only if they are of help in guiding us to intended experiences. If they are vague or confused, if the same word points to experiences that differ or run counter to each other, then language, instead of helping us, stands in our way. Mathematicians, in order to avoid these hindrances and pitfalls, long ago invented the languages of arithmetic and algebra for purposes of clear communication. More recently logicians, with the same purpose in mind, have devised the special language of symbolic logic. Dewey, stubbornly and laboriously, has used the common language to clarify his meanings. That is why so much of his writing is "difficult," studded as it is with qualifying clauses, qualified in turn, in order to state as precisely as possible what it is he has in mind.

To revert to our illustration of the word "knowledge." If, to two people engaged in conversation, it means something different —if, for example, it means mystical insight or revelation to one and scientific method to the other—they are talking at cross purposes. Nor, as we have observed, need there be anything immediately arbitrary about their respective choice of meanings. Down at the bottom the choice has to do, rather, with differing world views.

If on the one hand the ancient world view regarded knowledge as contemplation or mystical identification, while on the other science comprises the knowledge that gave us the modern world, then our language has to be redefined, reconstructed, in order to carry on consistently significant discourse in the modern world. Indeed, this is part of what it means to reconstruct our common sense: to start using language in more generally accepted ways, so that it reliably points to experiences that can be had in common. When such experiences are more general, when they are more genuinely common, they will further reshape that common sense which is our medium of exchange with each other, which is our means of communication.

Let us now close in on the problem. Important as language is, it is after all merely a tool of experience. Underlying it and following from it is experience itself. Experience is not only what we have, but what we are. The kinds of experiences each of us has largely determine what we become. The central thing about our social institutions is that, channeling individual experience along certain ways, they create certain kinds of individuals. Individuality is not something with which we are born. It is something we achieve in the course of a lifetime. That is why other people's pictures of what we are, to say nothing of our own private images of ourselves, are less statements of fact than goals toward which we tend. To put the matter paradoxically, the selves through which we live are creations of our living.

See where this takes us. Our self-images are products of experience. Experience, in turn, is shaped by our social institutions. Consequently, each of us in his own way strives to become what our culture tells us we ought to be. If we live in a unified culture, such as most primitive societies are, then we can ride smoothly down the stream of experience. If we live in a diversified culture, with multiple trends and countertrends, such as Western civilization was before the industrial revolution, then we must navigate the undercurrents and treacherous cross currents of experience more cautiously, but we gain a certain independence and self-reliance in the process. If, however, we live in a culture at odds with itself, such as ours is, with professed ideals often contradicting life-activities, then countless numbers of people will be smashed to bits in the whirlpools of experience. This is exactly what happens to millions of us, so that we speak with Karen Horney of "the neurotic personality of our time." Those who are emotionally crippled we institutionalize, in hospitals or prisons. Those who are less seriously injured we turn over to the psychiatrists and psychoanalysts. In a word, we treat sick individuals, as certainly we should, but we do so under the delusion that we are thus dealing with our problem. We are not. The problem is our disease-breeding institutional life and, in Lawrence K. Frank's telling words, society is the patient.

We have mentioned the contradictions between professed ideals and life-activities. They are commonplace enough. Just for that reason they are worth a moment's reflection. We raise our children with ideals of co-operation at the same time that we do everything we can to prepare them for a hard-boiled competitive world. We praise modesty and forbearance at the same time that we demonstrate that aggressive self-promotion is what pays off. We preach respect for law and order at the same time that we boast of "fixing" a traffic ticket or "taking care of" a government agent who examined our income-tax return. We insist that Christ died on the cross for all men at the same time that we make it plain that there are reservations with respect to Negroes, Chinese, Japanese, Filipinos, Mexicans, Indians, Mohammedans, Jews, Hindus, and communists. The list of contradictions goes on and on, and any one of us can lengthen it for as long as we savor the sport.

The point is that we know enough to distrust any man who talks out of both sides of his mouth at the same time. But our culture does just that. That is why we are confused and divided within ourselves, lost individuals in a world of conflict. For the orthodox religious tradition, salvation depends upon rising above the world. For Dewey, it depends upon reconstructing it.

Democracy is a tired word, but it still stands for a revolutionary idea. It stands for creating a new human potential as modern technology has created a new industrial potential. That is why the reconstruction required of us is a thoroughgoing one, not a piecemeal approach to this problem or that, but a complete overhauling. As we have observed, we have to see democracy itself, not merely as a political mechanism, but as an overarching moral ideal. We have to see human nature, not as limited and fixed, but infinitely malleable. We have to see experience, not as something distinct from man which nevertheless happens to him, but as the warp and woof of human existence. We have to see thinking, not as the voice of reason which somehow communes with truth, but as the method for solving problems. We have to see knowledge, not as a certain grasp of the immutable, but as relatively dependable propositions about a changing world. We have to see education, not as a fixed curriculum in the schools, but as a process that helps to create individuality—a process in which all our social institutions play a part.

The problem we have been discussing can be put another way. There is a basic split in democratic personality. On the one hand democracy on a continental scale would not be possible were it not for modern science, technology, and industry. On the other hand we bring to this industrial civilization minds grooved by preindustrial institutions, chiefly the institution of private enterprise. As a consequence, new inventions and industrial techniques are not looked at from the viewpoint of how they can best serve the general welfare. They are approached, rather, along the lines of a private-profit economy and, except when it is a matter of waging war, the primary question is always how they can best be used to yield the most profits.

Take the case of atomic energy. Government-sponsored re-search was pushed to successful practical conclusions as a war measure. Now, military men are technical specialists, and although some of them thought of the atom bomb merely as a more effi-cient weapon for carrying on warfare in the same old way, others knew immediately that its implications were revolutionary. To-day, only a few years after its introduction, we can see that the bomb brought with it radical changes in military strategy and tactics, and the experts are still feeling their way to find out what it means. Obviously, there is a world of difference between two schools of thought: between those whose minds were set and, when the bomb came, were clear about how *they* meant to use *it;* and those with creative imagination, determined to find out what *it* suggested about its own most effective use. It is the difference between the lumbering tank of World War I and the tank of the *Blitzkrieg* a generation later, the former being a new weapon fitted into accepted patterns of waging war, the latter an instru-ment for revolutionizing the conduct of war.

Although we are still a long way from it, the use of atomic energy for peaceful purposes is what most of us want. When the time does come, how is it to be used? Will it be put at the disposal of those with set minds, who know how they mean to use it, namely, for private profit? Or will it be raw material for creative imagination, seeking to learn what the new energy suggests about industrial reorganization?

This is not, at the moment, the abstract question whether private enterprise does or does not yield the greatest public bene-fit, a question leading so often to doctrinaire discussion. It is a question of the closed versus the open mind or, more accurately, of dogmatism versus scientific method. This is what we mean by the split in democratic personality. Modern industry, without which modern democracy would be impossible, grew out of that modern science which depends upon undogmatic minds, free intelligence. By and large, however, that very industry is manned, as well as directed and controlled, by minds committed to the dogma of the untouchable sanctity of private-profit enterprise.

This is the central dilemma to which Dewey has been calling our attention. He did not create it. Neither can he resolve it. But he has been tireless in trying to get us to focus our attention on it. For unless we do, the contradictions in our life will deepen until democracy itself is destroyed.

This is exactly the position of the extremists, the totalitarians both of the right and the left, that democracy will be destroyed by its internal contradictions. Those on the right, the fascists, would help the process along by seizing power in the name of a new era, gaining support from vested economic interests and a frightened middle class, but centralizing power in a party elite, a dictatorship. Those on the left, the communists, would help the process along by seizing power in the name of a "people's" democracy, gaining support from the "proletariat" and a section of the intelligentsia, but centralizing power in a party elite, a dictatorship. Each of them insists that the central dilemma cannot be resolved democratically, and their basic tactic, as they try to pave the way toward their own goals, is to undermine liberal democracy by sapping its faith in itself.

Right here lies Dewey's political significance. In his reappraisal and restatement of the meaning of liberal democracy, he has given vision and faith to untold numbers of people. Many of them, to be sure, have been recipients indirectly, at second or third hand, completely unaware of their indebtedness to his thinking, sometimes unaware even of his existence. That is as it should be for a philosophy with deep social roots, sensitive to human needs and conscious of human powers. How has he done this? What is his answer to the democratic dilemma? It is that liberalism itself can and must become radical. It must become radical in the exact sense of going to the root of the problem. The root of the problem is the intelligent use of modern technology in behalf of the broadest public welfare. And the democratic faith is that people can achieve this for themselves, indeed that unless they do achieve it for themselves it is unattainable, since democratically that is what the general welfare means.

Again, this may sound paradoxical. But it will sound so only to those of an absolutistic temper of mind, who have no genuine faith in people. For all such, however well-intentioned, there is a cocksure, dogmatic assumption that while the people may not know what is good for them, *they* know. They not only know, but they have every intention of seeing to it that the people get what is good for them—even if they have to run roughshod over them in the process. On a smaller scale, we can often see this attitude expressed in philanthropic work. It is the attitude of the professional "do-gooder" who, come hell or high water, is going to drum some good into others, whether they want it or not. The attitude is bad enough when it expresses itself on a small scale. When it dominates a nation, as we have tragically learned, it can become a scourge to all mankind.

Now, the general welfare, democratically conceived, necessarily involves the participation of all those who are affected by the processes at work in any situation. This is what we mean by the democratic use of the ballot, whereby the citizens with common concerns (whether municipal, statewide, or national) express their sentiments at the polls. It is for this reason that the disfranchisement of any group of the population, as is the case with Negroes in many parts of the South, is a practical deprivation of the rights of citizenship and is, as it always must be, an offense to democracy. Evidently, however, the casting of ballots in voting booths, important as it is, comes out to a minimum of democratic participation. It was for this reason that the direct primary election was instituted, so that affected citizens might express their views in the selection of candidates among whom a final decision is to be made. But this, too, is a limited degree of participation. That is why the old New England town meeting, where citizens with a daily experience of what they are talking about thrash out problems in face-to-face discussion, is the prime exemplification of political democracy. There seems to be no way of putting that principle to work nationally. Yet there can be no doubt that the closer we approximate it the more democratic will be our political life.

This business of active participation in affairs of common

concern is the crux of the matter. We can speak of it as a democratic "right," as we often do. As Dewey has pointed out in various ways, however, what we mean when we say it is that this is no mere expression or privilege of democracy. It *is* democracy. It rests on the belief that people living together this way, no matter what fool mistakes they may make, are in the long run better off than if they live any other way. The dogmatic extremists, of course, the absolutists, believe nothing of the sort. On the contrary, they believe, as we have said, that people must be saved from themselves. The trouble with absolutism, whether of the right or the left, whether political or religious, lies not in its goals or methods alone. It lies rather in the arbitrary disjunction it makes between goals and methods, between means and ends. It lies in the failure to realize that the way we try to achieve something is an inseparable part of whatever we achieve. When an athlete pole-vaults better than fourteen feet, his soaring that high is not an act complete in itself, separable from others. His running approach to the bar, his leaping takeoff, the way in which he hurls himself from the pole and swings his body, all these *are* the vault. Nor can the arduous self-discipline, the months of training and practice, be separated from it. So in all things. The goal is *in* the methods, the end is *in* the means. At least, this is the democratic belief, as nobody has spelled out more clearly than Dewey.

It is because of this ends-means relationship, because democratic goals cannot be separated from democratic methods, that the way we carry on our economic life looms so importantly in Dewey's social thinking. Believing as he does in multiple causation, that all kinds of institutions and attitudes shape what we are, he could not fall into the trap of the economic determinists, giving in general primacy in all times and places to economic factors, if not reducing everything to them. Yet at the same time this is true, the industrial organization of society both gives shape to modern democracy and creates its central problems. That is why, in our time, it is a matter of central concern. What are its implications?

We start with a political proposition, that in a democracy every citizen should participate in decisions that concern him. But political life does not exist in a vacuum. It is inextricably interwoven with other aspects of the common life—which is why, as Lincoln Steffens pointed out, no corrupt political machine can exist except in alliance with some vested economic interests. What is true institutionally is also true personally. We may think we can be one thing as citizens and another thing in the rest of our lives, but in the long run we fool no one but ourselves. Our dominant patterns of behavior manifest themselves in all our activities.

Now, it is not enough, if political democracy is to function successfully, for citizens to participate in affairs. They must participate intelligently, responsibly. That means that they must have a pattern of intelligent and responsible behavior. Theoretically, that is what our educational system is calculated to achieve, and its successes and failures cannot be judged apart from this. But we know that all our lives are subject to the dominating influence of our economic institutions. Even those not directly involved in them, such as housewives and children, are nonetheless powerfully influenced by the attitudes they engender.

What attitudes, then, what patterns of behavior are inculcated by our economic life? They are manifold, of course, but primary among them is one of boss-worker relations. The man on top—owner, manager, engineer, supervisor, or whatever—is accustomed to giving orders to those underneath, and he expects those orders to be carried out. In large measure, business "efficiency" rests on just this system of relations. The good executive is commonly regarded as one who can make quick, sound decisions about what is to be done, give clear instructions to his subordinates, and see that those instructions are followed. The good worker is one who understands his instructions, accepts them readily, and carries them out promptly. It will probably be more gratifying to all concerned if executives and workers have a good, that is a friendly, human relation, and most executives like to preen themselves on how well they get along with "their" men. Yet this is by no means an essential of the enterprise. What is really essential is that the work get done, and no nonsense. "Non-sense" is when workers try to get out of line by saying what is to be done and how it is to be done. Gradually, an increasing amount of this "nonsense" has had to be tolerated because of the growing strength of labor unions. But then, within many of the unions, the same pattern is duplicated, with executives holding a tight rein on the rank and file. In brief, notwithstanding welcome changes in recent years, the dominant pattern of our economic life is a boss-bossed relation.

Workers, however, are not one thing on their jobs and another thing as citizens. Is it any wonder, then, that our political life has been dominated by machine bosses?

Obviously, despite the relative well-being we have enjoyed as a nation, genuine political democracy cannot exist unless democratic relations characterize the common life, unless democracy is a way of life. The large amount of political democracy we have had has been tied to other democratic influences at work in society. But as our central dilemma sharpens, as industrial life draws more of us and more of everything into its orbit, the more crucial become its patterns of behavior. Compared with this, problems of wages and hours, of working conditions, of job security, of pensions—important as they are—nevertheless occupy a peripheral position. The need of liberal democracy is industrial democracy. Industrial democracy, despite pontifical declarations to the contrary, rests on the intelligent and responsible participation of all those concerned. That is why Dewey, devoted as he is to the experimental method, has never been so experimental as to be spineless in his approach to our central problem. He knows enough to know that human experimentalism did not begin with his writing books about it. And even though the future cannot and should not be blueprinted, even though there will be misses as well as hits in the course of future experimentation, he believes we do have sound indications of the directions democracy must take.

In order to be clear about these directions, however, we have first to see more clearly the basic facts of our economic life.

Traditionally, private enterprise has justified itself on three grounds. The starting point is the contention that if every man follows his own interest and minds his own business, the common interest will best be served. The free market will function so that there will be automatic adjustments of supply and demand, prices and wages, investment and profits. Business will flourish, labor prosper; more goods will be produced, more goods consumed; and all will be for the best in the best of all possible economic worlds.

The theory assumes that business will neither want nor brook any intervention by government, for by definition that would be a violation of the free market—but businessmen have belied the theory by taking government help, in the form of tariffs and subsidies, whenever they could get it. The theory assumes that business will relish a system of competition open to all comers, for otherwise there is no free market—but businessmen have belied the theory by suppressing competition, through trade agreements and trusts, whenever they could. The theory assumes that business will want to produce as much as it can at all times, for this is the meaning of the free market—but businessmen have belied the theory by limiting production whenever it is financially profitable to do so. The theory assumes that whenever there are temporary dislocations in the free market (deflation or depression), the masses of people will quietly tide themselves over the uncomfortable period—but the people have belied the theory by increasingly intense resentment over the human misery it entails.

On this point, therefore, the facts are clear. The theory of the free market is untenable because business will not accept it and no government responsive to the attitudes of the people will risk it.

The second ground on which private enterprise has justified itself has been its theory of human nature. It is claimed that, however regrettable it may be, human beings are motivated by self-interest. Self-interest in economics is best expressed in private gain, in other words through the profit motive. If we agree with

Dewey's theory of human nature, however, recognizing its plasticity and seeing it as an expression of various culture patterns and emphases, we are forced to reject the claim. On the record, whether we do or do not agree with Dewey, there is enough psychological and anthropological evidence available to refute the self-interest theory.

The third justification of private enterprise has generally been taken to be the most convincing, and until recent years there were none but theoretical refutations of it. It is the claim that, no matter what we think of the free market or human nature or anything else, the system of private enterprise has brought the world untold riches. One might even be willing to face squarely the vast misery that had followed in its wake and yet, in balance, admit that this tragic price was worth paying for the incalculable benefits that also came out of it. There has been no denying the riches, any more than there is any disputing the fact that the standard of living of the masses of people has steadily risen. And if all this has indeed come from the system of private enterprise, what better justification could anyone want?

It has seemed heretical, not to say a little bit softheaded, to deny it. Even the most virulent critics of the system, the Marxists, agreed that this was the case; and their "scientific" socialism has rested on the proposition that, having served its purpose and served it well, private enterprise is now outmoded and so rent by internal contradictions that it cannot continue. Yet this heresy of denial is exactly the position that Dewey, with Veblen, has maintained. The tremendous material gains in the past century, he insists, have been due, not to private enterprise, but to modern technology. They are not the same. Neither do they have any necessary relation to each other. There was private enterprise before there was modern technology. No one could dispute this. But there can also be modern technology without private enterprise. Until the present day, this was only "theory," and no hardheaded realist could put any stock in it. Now we have the example of the Soviet Union staring us in the face, and regardless of how much we may dislike it, we cannot blink it away. For whatever else the Soviet Union is or is not, it assuredly is not a private-enterprise economy. Nevertheless, in the space of thirty years, this nation of peasants has become an industrial giant capable of producing the atom bomb.

Yes, we live in an industrial civilization. Within it, however, and playing a dominant role over it, there has been a business civilization. Mostly, because of inertia, lack of analysis, and subtle propaganda, we have confused the two, thinking that business *is* industry. It is not. And recognition of the fact that it is not is Dewey's handle to resolving our central dilemma. It may well be that business civilization is doomed. That would not be the end of democracy. On the contrary, it might clear the way for the further realization of our democratic potential. For democracy's necessary relation is to modern industry. As people come to know this more and more, they may devise the techniques that will end the business control of industrial civilization and give increasing effect to the ideal of industrial democracy.

As a matter of fact, we have been so blinded by our unexamined common sense that we have kept on talking about private enterprise when the bulk of it is not private at all. Most of it is public enterprise, controlled by individuals for their own benefit, for private ends. But this is quite another thing.

The distinction between private and public is one of the most important distinctions we have to make. Stated simply, "private" is what concerns ourselves, "public" is what concerns others as well as ourselves. Strictly speaking, of course, no hard-and-fast lines can be drawn between the two. When we tell a story to members of our family, for example, we are engaged in a public act; yet we also say significantly that what happens in our families is part of our private lives. On the other hand, even if he resents it, the private life of a President of the United States is a matter of public concern—not just curiosity, but genuine concern, for what he is privately cannot be separated from what he is publicly, and what he is can make a good deal of difference to all the rest of us. The degree of difference a given act makes to other people, and the number and kinds of people who have a genuine concern in it, are what give us our practical distinction between private and public.

Because different people can be concerned in many of the same things, and the same people can be concerned in many different things, Dewey points out that there are many "publics." So with respect to economic matters, "the" public really consists of many different and frequently overlapping publics. This is one major reason why it is not desirable to try to blueprint plans for industrial democracy. Different branches of industry have the responsibility for working out the implications of their concern. That is something that no one person, no group of persons, and no government ought to try to do for them.

In the light of these considerations, let us take another look at our central dilemma. The dilemma is how modern industry, originating in free intelligence but dominated by the dogma of private enterprise, is ever going to solve its problems democratically. The first part of the answer is to rid ourselves of the dogma, which we have seen is without rational justification. The second part of the answer is to determine, just as imaginative militarists have tried to do with the atom bomb, what the industrial system itself indicates about its most effective use.

Obviously, the industrial system has its primary meaning in its ability to turn out many goods quickly and cheaply. Aside from anything else, therefore, certainly that is what it should be used to do. Whatever stands in the way of this is undesirable and unintelligent.

Next, there is no point in turning out many goods quickly and cheaply unless they are made easily available to as many people as possible. Looked at in this way, the meaning of the industrial system is the multiplication of benefits for the consuming public, so that efficiency of production in the last analysis is to be judged by the consumer. Whatever stands in the way of this is undesirable and unintelligent.

Finally, and most important of all, the meaning of the industrial system lies in its potential educative force as an instrument of democracy. On the face of it, modern industry would not be possible without the co-operative efforts of vast numbers of people. If democracy is co-operative participation, which it is, and industry is co-operative, which it is, then the indicated next step is obvious. The co-operation on which industry depends must be converted into the genuine participation of all those involved. This means the ending of the boss-bossed relation, whatever administrative mechanisms are devised for dealing with different situations. It means that executives, in management and labor unions alike, will have to stop being dictators and start being agents of whatever public their activities involve. It means that workers, instead of being "hands" or robots on a belt line, will have to become persons with a feeling of responsibility on their jobs. It means that consumers, instead of taking pot luck at the businessman's table, will have to have something to say about what's to be served for dinner.

In a word, the answer to our central dilemma, both economically and democratically, lies in responsible participation in co-operative enterprise.

This is the essence of Dewey's social philosophy. Granted the necessity for endless experimentation, there is no doubt that to his mind co-operative enterprise is clearly intelligent and good. It is intelligent because it is indicated by the nature of modern industry itself; because it would resolve the contradictions that threaten to destroy democracy; and because it would put government in its proper place as a helpful resource available to people as they need it, preventing it from becoming an instrument of coercion or oppression. It is good because it is intelligent; because it would prevent society from hardening into class lines, the antithesis of democracy; and because it would liberate the minds and personalities of countless individuals to make their creative contributions to the common life.

We can put the matter another way. We are often inclined to think of economic determinism as some strange and foreign import, even though Madison, the father of our constitution, was writing about it before Karl Marx was born. Whether native or foreign-born, however, it is something with which we have to come to terms. For as Dewey has said, it is now a fact and not a theory. It is a fact, not in the sense in which it is sometimes used, that all social processes are finally reducible to economic terms. It is a fact, rather, in another, twofold sense. First, as we have seen, the way in which we live our economic life has a good deal to do with our general patterns of behavior. Second, the point of economic development which we have now reached defines, or determines, the possibilities that are open to us. Those possibilities, for Dewey, fall within one category. He believes that, whatever we call it, co-operative enterprise of one kind or another is here to stay. Ours is the choice of the kind we are to have. It is a choice between a co-operative enterprise that is privately controlled for purposes of private profit and one that is publicly controlled in the public interest. To choose the former, actively or by default, is to continue science as a tool of vested interests, in which intelligence is put to work in behalf of ends already set for it. To choose the latter is to free intelligence for creative work in determining and achieving common ends.

This is what freedom is. That what has already happened limits our possibilities and determines the scope of our choices is no infringement on our freedom, let alone a denial of it. For the meaning of freedom lies not in what precedes it, but in what follows from it. The ability to choose among the alternatives before us is a measure of the freedom we now have. If we are intelligent enough to choose wisely, we shall multiply our choices and increase our freedom in the days to come.

If we choose wisely, our places of employment will be converted from places where we earn a living into places where we live significant lives. If we choose wisely, the geographic areas in which we reside will be converted into neighborhoods in which we share enriching experiences with those who are our neighbors. To do these things is to build communities in which people with much in common can have that free communication that sometimes culminates in the communion of one spirit with another. Such communion as this may or may not be holy. But surely it is the point at which democracy, as a way of life, becomes religious experience.

# CHAPTER FIVE

# ON FIRST AND LAST THINGS

"SHARED experience is the greatest of human goods."

If there is one sentence that compresses into itself all that Dewey has thought and said, this is it. It gives point to his psychology, his logic, his sense of philosophy as a criticism of criticisms. It pulls together what he means by education, by democracy, by ethics, by aesthetics, and by religion.

These are little words, each of them, and yet they stretch in their abstractness to cover multitudes. How are we to localize them? How are we to find the ways to say them? Through other words, leading to still other words, only to be enmeshed finally in a tangled skein of verbiage? Doubtless this is the way with some. It is not the way of those who try to feel the pulse-beats of experience itself. There is a point at which all language is but a dumbshow, pantomiming in its own terms what experience would be if we had it. The thing is to have it.

What were the experiences of Shakespeare? None of us knows or will ever know; not merely because of the little knowledge we have of him, but because even if he were our contemporary the "facts" of his life would not give us the feel of experience for him. Yet, in a deeper sense, we do know what experience was for him, because of what he has communicated to us.

What does this mean? At a certain stage in his life, this incredible man reads the chronicle of Hamlet. He does not transcribe it, as a chronicler would, nor engage in extensive research, as a historian. He transfuses it with his own imaginative power, until Hamlet is the child of his creation. Over the years, one great actor after another plays the part. No, "plays" is not the word. For each of them in his turn, in his own way, creates his Hamlet. Poet and actor have had a creative relation to each other, an interrelation. Generations pass, the motion picture is invented and rapidly reaches high levels of technical development, when another actor, Laurence Olivier, is taken with an idea. He puts Hamlet on the screen, creating now not only a new Hamlet but a new work of art. The rest of us, seeing it, do not sit passive before it. We bring to it our experiences, our passions and frustrations, our tensions and guilts, our lies and loves, and so much else never to be articulated and sometimes only dimly felt. Not just Shakespeare, then, creates his Hamlet. Not just Olivier. No, each of us creates his own, sharing with them in a creative process.

After we have "seen" it, if we say anything at all, we are as likely as not to say, "What an experience!" How can we tell another what we mean? We cannot. We may verbalize about it, but in all candor we should say, "That's an experience you'll just have to have for yourself."

Out of the jungle of possible sounds, a Beethoven captures some. They surge through him relentlessly, overpowering him, until it is impossible to say which is capturer and which captive. Notes tumble out of his brain onto the paper, and in the process an orchestra is converted into the voice of titans. But he does not need an entire orchestra. A single instrument will do. And the piano alone becomes that voice. A century later, a Schnabel becomes the master of an incomparable piano technique. He picks up the scores of the Beethoven sonatas and asks himself, in effect, what the composer meant by them. Obviously, he cannot answer that. All the brooding power and enchantment of the one, all the tenderness and bitterness, all the tragedy and ongoing affirmation are inert, are merely potentials, without the creative genius of the other. Yet again, it is not Schnabel who brings them alive for us. We participate with him, or else the notes might just as well result in dead sounds falling on dead ears. And when we say,

"You haven't heard the Beethoven sonatas until you've heard Schnabel play them. What an experience!", we are saying something about ourselves as well as about them.

What we are saying about ourselves, according to Dewey, is that we are actively involved in whatever is "an" experience for us. Experience, as we have seen, is the stuff of life. As far as human beings are concerned, there is no meaningful sense in which there is anything beyond experience, outside it, with which it can be compared or contrasted. Whatever has any genuine meaning for us is, by definition, part of experience. Experience, therefore, in all its breadth and depth, its flux and uncertainty, has, if not an anonymity, an impersonal quality about it. "Things" happen. And when, about certain things, we say that they did not just *happen,* meaning that they were "caused" by certain preceding things, we have simply identified them as part of a continuous process, and have not necessarily made experience any more or less personal.

For example, when rain comes, we carefully say "*It* is raining." If we are meteorologists, we will not say that it just happened to rain. Instead, if called upon, we will go into an analysis of cloud formations, wind velocities and directions, cold and hot climatic fronts, and any other relevant data, to show *why* it is raining. After the explanation as before, however, the rain retains its same impersonal character.

Now, when a professional rainmaker goes to work, sending airplanes up to "seed" the clouds, even when he is successful it would not occur to him to say, "*I* rain." If he did, he would be ridiculed, or perhaps institutionalized. And yet, as a matter of plain fact, if he actually did have anything to do with it, he occupies a different relation to this rain than he does to a "natural" rainfall. Nevertheless, the relation he does occupy is of an instrumental character. He was putting certain bits of knowledge to work in order to achieve a certain end.

When we talk about "an" experience, on the other hand, there is an altogether different relation involved, and an altogether different feel about it. One might say to a friend, for example: "Golly, did I have an experience in that rain last night! Just when the downpour started, I remembered that I'd left my car in the street with the windows open. I dashed out of the house, closed them, and wasn't five steps away from the car again when a bolt of lightning sent a tree crashing down on top of it. I stood there with my mouth open, thinking about what would have happened to me if I'd been thirty seconds later. Did I take a stiff drink when I got back in the house!" In this case, a portion of the anonymous flux of experience has become personalized in a unique way. It is the kind of situation about which a story can be told, a story with a beginning, a development, a climax—and even an anticlimax. In a word, it is no longer just experience. It is, stated quite accurately, "an" experience.

The endless flux of experience, evidently, is not a meaningless welter. It has its phases, even as the seasons have, and it waxes and wanes, even as the moon does. Dewey is by no means the first to have called attention to this rhythmic character of nature. But he made a contribution of singular importance when, having emphasized that experience *is* nature, he went on to show what it is for experience to have phases: tensions and releases, beginnings and endings, introductions and culminations. He thereby restored art to nature, and he became a prophet of the day when, in industrial civilization, beauty will cease to be a museum piece and will become part of the ordinary experience of ordinary men and women.

So far can misunderstanding go, however, that some of those who have been most impatient with the rest of Dewey's philosophy, and even contemptuous of it, have been unstinting in their appreciation and praise of his philosophy of art. For anyone who has ever caught the center of Dewey's vision, this is almost incomprehensible. There is a point of view, not the least important, from which we can say that his philosophy of art *is* his philosophy.

"An" experience, as we have seen, is experience individualized, personalized. It is what it is, unique, induplicable. Because it is, it is fleeting, and we can never be certain that it will come

or that, in coming, it will be what we thought it might be. Santayana, with much the same set of data, draws different conclusions, constructing an elaborate philosophy of essences which is
impressed not so much with the fleeting character of such qual-
itative experiences as these as it is with the persistence of their
meanings once they have occurred. This is not Dewey's concern.
That meanings persist does not signify that they persist un-
changed, as we know from the fact that those who have been
close to us and are now dead often mean different things to us
at different stages of our own lives. However that may be, the
persistence of meanings is, in any event, beyond our control.
Their occurrence, their creation, is not.

As the very meaning of life is to be found in the richness of
the meanings experience unfolds, so our concern must be with
creating the conditions under which desirable meanings can occur.
We need tools in order to create them—tools of inquiry, of education, of production, of communication—but the tools are that,
and nothing more. The meaning of the tools lies in the meanings
they make available to us. We need general principles by means
of which to carry on the business of life. But the business of life
is not with general principles. It is with individual, individualized,
experiences. So the artist needs brushes and palette with which
to paint, but the finished canvas is the meaning of his work. And
as in all other aesthetic experiences, the picture we see, the thing
that gives us "an" experience, is neither on the canvas alone nor
in us alone. It is rather in a unique interaction of the two which
makes it *our* experience. We say "our" to show our personal
stake in it, when in reality it possesses us as much as we possess
it. Yet, to put the whole matter another way, our personal stakes
in experience are what the human enterprise is all about.

When Dewey urges us to go to the arts to learn what experience is, accordingly, he is telling us what his philosophy is all
about. If we exclaim, "What an experience!" in connection with
a Hamlet, a Beethoven sonata, a Michelangelo sculpture, or a
Vermeer painting, we are pointing at both a failure and a consummation. The failure lies in the inadequacy of words to com-

municate on this level: for if words were found to communicate what we mean, they would actually be communicating something else of their own, comprising another experience, perhaps a poem, as in Keats's *Ode on a Grecian Urn*. The consummation is the achievement of genuine communication. Whatever says itself in its own terms, unduplicably, is an ideal merger of instrument and end, as when a great singer, using his voice to bring us music, actually demonstrates that the use of the voice *is* the music. Such an experience is a compound of many things—a portion of the otherwise anonymous flux, the creator, our participating selves, tension and release, consummation and satiety—all somehow integrated, giving a sense of harmony, of nothing more needing to be done or said.

That all this is involved in an experience of art does not make it any different in kind from "an " experience of any other sort, such as a narrow escape from death in a rainstorm. On the contrary, it shows that "an" experience, as a point of concentration in the general flux, is capable of becoming a point of unification, of satisfaction, of prized meanings. This is not what life is, a matter of prized meanings. But it is what life can increasingly become if, as we say, we use our heads. Thus we see clearly what Dewey means by the instrumental function of intelligence, logic, knowledge: through ceaseless experiment to find out ever better ways of using our heads for the achievement of prized meanings.

But what meanings are to be prized? It is hard to think of a single experience which, one way or another, sooner or later, has not been prized or might not be prized by someone. Are they all, then, on the same level? Is there no difference between the meanings prized by saints and scoundrels, no method of choosing among them?

Much of the future of the human race depends upon the answers to these questions. As a matter of fact, the resolution of that central dilemma of democracy, which we have discussed, is involved in them. For unless enough people want deeply enough to follow the path of publicly controlled co-operative enterprise, it will never be followed. Yet who is to say that it *should* be followed, that it is *better* to follow it than some alternative path? Grant even that it is the intelligent thing to do, why be intelligent? History is studded with the betrayals of intelligence, and recent history not least of all. It used to be said that passion blinds the reason. Now it is fashionable to blame our neuroses. In either event, intelligence is castrated. Meanwhile, those entrenched in a narrow self-interest try cynically to exploit the rest of us, and those with a conviction of their own divine mission threaten and cajole us in the effort to herd us to salvation.

The big word in our time is "relativity." And the big problem in ethical philosophy is the relativity of morals. Ironically enough, the problem would never have arisen, in all its besetting human implications, were it not for the freeing of intelligence and modern inquiries into human behavior. For the old dogmatic morality, which was rooted in absolutism, had its fruit in those guardians of heaven who issued fiats about what was required of man. The higher criticism of the Bible, the scientific grounding of evolution theory, and studies in comparative religion and folkways combined with the earlier movements of Protestant and economic individualism to shatter the dogma of revelation and its authority over conduct.

Both individually and socially, therefore, the confusions of a revolutionary age became the matrix of moral confusion, of ethical relativism. Individually, a person's behavior was regarded as a function of his family background, his social status, his religious affiliation, his emotional complexes—an accident of biography or, if you will, a matter of arbitrary preference, of taste. Since there is no arguing about tastes, every man thus becomes a law unto himself, provided he does not violate social regulations. Socially, behavior was seen as an expression of the peculiar configurations of a culture, and since each culture "knows" best how to get along in its own situation, there is no common criterion to be used among them.

Whatever the theoretical supports for such relativism as this, the upshot of it is literally intolerable. Individuals, as we know from psychiatric studies, can be destroyed if they are raised without standards; or, putting it more accurately, they can be prevented from attaining any stable individuality. Moral confusion so widespread and devastating as this cannot be borne, and one answer to it is the resurgence of absolutism. Almost in panic the various objections to absolutism are cast side in exchange for the "security" of being told what to do by a church or a political party. The unbearable burden of this relativism is even more manifest socially. For in the last analysis, if there is no rational ground for choosing among the standards of different cultures, and they clash, they must resort to the arbitrament of force. Under these circumstances, although might surely does not make right, it just as surely determines what is to be regarded as right. If this were a theoretical matter, and nothing more, it would be bad enough. When it becomes the theoretical justification for the blood torrents of our time, its logic is race suicide.

Now there is a sense in which moral relativism is an indisputable fact, one which, as we have seen, is embraced in Dewey's conception of human nature. As even a superficial acquaintance with comparative ethnology makes clear, the moral ideas of mankind vary from culture to culture. Obviously, therefore, there is nothing innate in human beings which makes their morality the same, regardless of time and place. Neither does a universal dictum, laid down by some transcendent power or in some other transcendent fashion, hold sway over the minds of men. Morality is relative to the conditions in which it arises, as the free play of a piston is relative to the cylinder in which it moves.

To be aware of this is important in several respects. First, it is a tool to better understanding of what is involved in any prevailing system of morality. Second, it is an excellent antidote for arrogant self-righteousness. Third, it drives home to us the fact that changes in conditions can produce concomitant changes in morality, giving us a handle that may some day enable us to raise the level of human relations.

To understand that moral ideas are relative to the culture in which they arise, however, does not require that we submit to that other species of relativism which is really a state of ethical

anarchy. It is one thing to understand a situation. It is quite another thing to approve or disapprove of it, to accept or reject it.
Interpreted in one way, "To understand all is to forgive all" is
probably as blatant a bit of nonsense as one person ever parroted
from another. The better we understand some things, such as
Hitler's determination to rule or ruin, the more we abominate
them. To understand that crime is the result of emotional difficulties and environmental conditions is not to "accept" crime or
"justify" the criminal. Such understanding will affect our treatment of the criminal and the ways in which we approach the environment, but unless we have completely lost our senses, we will
still want to eradicate, or at least minimize, crime. So with moral
systems. That they have arisen in certain varying ways does not
justify the continuing existence of any one of them nor all of
them together. For in this, as in other things, the justification is
to be found, not in the antecedents, but in the consequences.

Is there any way, then, to choose among different systems
of morality? When one says that he believes democracy is better
than fascism, freedom better than authoritarianism, is he expressing merely a preference? Or is there an objective basis for choosing one rather than the other? Yes, there is such a basis, a basis
whose validity is to be determined in the living. The basis is the
actual results to which a system leads as judged by its own
purposes.

When a man and a woman marry, for example, they do so in
order to fulfill certain needs each of them brings to the situation.
It does not matter whether their needs correspond to the needs
of the couple next door or to those of any other couple they ever
heard about. What does matter is that their own individual needs,
or a reasonable proportion of them, be satisfied. If they are, the
marriage is a successful one. If they are not, then the marriage is
a failure, even if it does not terminate in divorce.

Now in our culture, when we speak of marriage, we mean
a monogamous relationship. What about polygamy? Within a
polygamous relationship, success or failure would again have to
be judged in terms of the satisfaction of needs.

How about choosing between monogamy and polygamy? This is a more seeming than real question, for in our experience, with minor exceptions, there have been no serious confrontations of one with the other. One thinks of the fate of polygamy among the Mormons in this country as substantiating evidence. In the populous East and Midwest, the overwhelming sentiment against their polygamous practices drove them out of the community. Finally, they found shelter in Utah, living unmolested there until the westward movement of population and of monogamous morality caught up with them. Then, once and for all, they were obliged to conform to the prevailing custom.

Suppose, however, that they had not been obliged to conform. Apart from theological and traditional considerations, how would one have chosen between monogamy and polygamy? Again, it would have had to be in the light of the comparative satisfaction of needs. In this case, of course, the perspective would have to be widened. The needs now to be considered, in a comparison of the two systems, would be those of the children as well as spouses, of families as units in relation to each other, of the community as a whole in its economic and civil life. If it could be shown that all the relevant human needs were satisfied in one system as well as in the other, then, whatever our preconceptions, there would be no moral difference between them. If it could be shown, on the contrary, that the results of monogamous relations are decisively favorable to the human needs involved, then it would be evident that monogamy is *really,* that is objectively, better than polygamy.

The dominant trends of any moral system are to be evaluated in just this way, despite the vastly greater complexity of the process. The justification for any system of morality, regardless of its origin, is to be found in the degree to which it satisfies the needs of the community, the degree to which it forwards the life-interests of its individual members. A morality that leaves no man secure with his neighbor, that gives no family security with other families, is no morality at all, or at least not one that could long survive.

All primitive societies of which we have any knowledge make rigorous demands on the conduct of their members. Without such demands, or standards of conduct, communal life is impossible. And even though, on primitive levels, no holds are barred with those outside the tribe, this is because the community itself is confined to the tribe. To be sure, there have been cultural lags, in morality as in other things, and customs, which once had an environmental or some other justification that has disappeared, persist simply because "our people have always done things this way." If such a cultural lag is serious enough, or if there are enough of them, the group may "moralize" itself into extinction.

Now, on simple levels of existence, moral systems are instruments of community survival and nothing more, no matter what their rationalizations may be. Nor is there likely to be much questioning either of the basis or the validity of the prevailing system. Complexities are introduced when differing tribes are in close proximity to each other and in constant contact. Then, sooner or later, if they are not to exterminate each other, they must find some way of living together, devise some system of intertribal morality. Till now, the human race has been so unsuccessful in doing this that our present-day morality of international relations remains on an aboriginal level. No doubt, with the instruments of destruction now at our disposal, this is why we have such grave misgivings about the survival of the race. So we see that even on the most complicated levels of existence, as well, morality is an instrument of survival. When we reach the point of creating that international community which is now a technical possibility, we shall require a moral system broad enough, and human enough, to satisfy the needs and forward the life-interests of its individual members.

But what does all this have to do with the question of choosing between democracy and fascism, freedom and authoritarianism? For Dewey, it is inseparably related with the idea of community itself. A community, we have said, exists because people who are able to communicate with each other are able to hold things in common, this in turn advancing their ability to communicate, and so on and on. Yet genuinely to hold something in common with another is freely to manifest an interest or concern of one's own. To be forced to have things in common is not really to have them at all, but to be subjected to them, ruled by them, as when a person, threatened by an armed attacker, grapples with him and together with him holds onto the gun for dear life. To have things in common, instead of being had by them, is to have that freedom of expression of which words are only the tools and the creative relation of one individuality to another is the end. To achieve this is to pursue the intelligent path of satisfying needs and life-interests. To have this is to have community. To have this is also to have democracy.

Community and democracy, being for Dewey practically equivalent terms, are a basic value. Does this have anything to do with intelligence? Do facts have anything to do with values, science with morality? If we examine the recent literature of ethical philosophy, we see how the controversy rages, and how the contention that one ought to have an integral relation with the other is met with thunderous denials and denunciations. There is, evidently, a vested interest in ideas as well as in other things. If this were not the case, the vigor with which a sharp dualism between science and values is defended would be hard to understand. As Dewey has observed, the only upshot of stressing the limits of science is the glorification of ignorance.

Values, after all, are simply what we prize. Offhand, one might think that the methods by which we try to get what we prize and by which we try to keep what we prize once we have it are inseparable from whatever is prized. To have daydreams about a girl one wants to marry, but to make no efforts to know her better in order to determine if one's want is valid or, if one feels sure enough about that, to court her—this is not to have a value. It is the sheerest sentimentality, what we commonly call the calf-love of a moonstruck youth.

This being a commonplace, one wonders what all the philosophic shooting is for. The answer is that, whatever their protestations to the contrary, many of those who sharply separate science and values do not do so on the basis of experience at all. Instead of doing this, they bring to experience an intellectual system that has already put facts in one world and values in another, and then they plague themselves and everyone else with sophisticated conundrums about how the two different worlds are related. Their reasons for doing this vary. On the whole, however, it seems that they all come down to the quest for certainty. It is the old desire for assurance that however things may go in this world, the things one values most (beauty, goodness, truth, love, righteousness, or whatever) are pegged down once and for all, somehow, somewhere. If a person needs this kind of reassurance, not much can be done about it.

It is probable, though not demonstrable in discussion, that the need for security in some hypothetical other world stems from the genuine insecurities of this one. If this is true, then the creation of a social order in which human beings experienced a reasonable degree of security here and now would dissipate the quest for certainy and liquidate the dualism between facts and values. In other words, it would be shown that the problem is not one of philosophy. It would be apparent, instead, that it is a problem of social action. Which is what Dewey has been saying all along.

Yet there are those who will say that we have not really touched the philosophic question involved, that we have simply skirted it. They will not deny that facts, intelligence, and science have an instrumental relation to values. They will rather agree that these are essential tools for seeing how to get what we want and for going ahead to get it. The point for them is that *what* we get is altogether different from *how* we get it, ends from means, values from facts. A man may want fifty millions dollars more than he wants anything else in the world. *Why* he wants it is part of his biography. Perhaps it is one consequence of his childhood relation with his father, or a need for power which he is convinced only a fortune will bring him, or an intuition that he was destined to be a financial tycoon. What does this have to do with science? The truths of science are attained by methods that have nothing whatever in common with the ways in which we get our values.

There is enough valid description of experience here to give us pause. Without doubt, there is an arbitrariness about the values most of us hold, and this arbitrariness itself is one of the brute facts of experience. In origin, therefore, our values seem to have no relation to intelligence—except (and a mighty important exception it is!) for whatever funded intelligence is already in our culture and our individual upbringing, since it is here that our values, too, are born and bred. But beyond this, one would have to grant that intelligence bears no necessary relation to values. We may want whatever we want, just so, and want it stubbornly, so that no evidence and no argument could ever dissuade us from it. Certainly there are people like that. A few of them turn out to be geniuses. The overwhelming mass of them, however, are simply behaving foolishly.

For the rest of us, it is a matter of course to bring to bear whatever intelligence we can, not only on the ways to get what we want, but also in trying to judge whether what we originally wanted is worth getting. The man who starts out by wanting fifty million dollars may canvass the situation a little more carefully. He may find that while a person with that much money has a great deal of social, political, or industrial power, he nevertheless in his private life is a prisoner to his fortune. He may find that possessing that much money will bring a man hangers-on instead of friends, envy instead of affection. Taking these and other things into consideration, he may then change his mind, his value; perhaps concluding that he will settle for one million dollars instead of fifty, perhaps taking another turn altogether. This may seem a trivial illustration. Yet nothing in life is more apparent than the ways in which one value is weighed in the scale against others and how, in the process, instead of simply choosing one over the others, we often emerge with a new value.

This is what we mean by judgment: the intelligent, understanding appraisal of conflicting values, the ability to penetrate to the heart of a problem in terms of its human import. The wise man is not just the learned man or the "knowing" man. He is the man of judgment. Without intelligence there is no judgment.

Let us agree that intelligence is not science. We have seen, however, that it is not different in kind from science, that science is organized intelligence, organized in its methods and organized socially. And even though we have no guarantees, still we have no valid reason to doubt that the emerging sciences of human behavior may yet eventuate in a science of human relations, in such a good marriage of science and values that it will bring the two ever closer with the passage of the years.

All this, stated so generally, is not to be understood as having merely a general significance. Nothing is more important to Dewey than the individuation of experience, and the point of using intelligence in human relations is that there be an increasing richness in individual lives. Yet neither general principles nor social conditions alone can bring that to pass. The individual himself has to be involved in it. We are reminded of our earlier paradox, that the individual creates himself in the process of expressing himself. That comes about through the choices we make in our day-to-day living. What we are deciding when we choose between two conflicting values, between alternative courses of action, is what kind of characters we want to have, what kind of persons we mean to be. We do not simply learn by doing. We *become* by doing. And if we are sufficiently aware of the nature of what we are, then the social roots of every self will have their fruits in the social consequences of what we choose to do and be. Here we can see the relation of morality as cultural survival with morality as individual choice. Whatever we choose to do and be, whether we wish it or not, eddies out from us far beyond the furthest point we shall ever see.

The moral person for Dewey, then, is one who not only understands this intellectually, but has a constant awareness of it in the choices he makes. He is one who is so sensitive to the social implications of what he chooses to do that it is the very atmosphere of his thinking and acting. We might call this moral consciousness, keeping in mind its outer as well as its inner dimensions. Or we might recast a theologically loaded term and call it conscience: conscience now naturalized, both at home in nature and giving nature as welcoming a home as any child should ever give its parents.

We talk about the self. Each of us is many things, pushes and pulls, ambitions and frustrations, tendencies and counter-tendencies. Where are we to discover the self we talk about so easily? The more we ponder the matter, the more elusive the self becomes, as when we try to grasp a globule of quicksilver between our fingers. Who knows better than ourselves what our selves are? And how much do we know? The selves we talk about, in truth, are not so much existents as intentions. *We* exist, all right, but the "we" is this complex we have just mentioned. The self as a completely integrated being, as a harmonious unity, is what we aim to become. Imaginatively, we project ourselves into the future, giving this natural organism we now are an ideal development it might then have. The self, on analysis, is seen to be an ideal. It is not an ideal dwelling in some never-never land. It is a working ideal, one which has the power increasingly to unify whatever we are through the active choices we make. It gives us a perspective from which we can better judge where we are in the light of where we are heading. What is true of the self is true of a collection of selves, of society. It is just that—a collection, except as it is unified in the light of shared ideals.

All the age-long controversies between materialism and idealism, accordingly, are for Dewey just vicious dualism all over again, the artificial cleaving of things that belong together, with human frustration as a consequence. Let us stop talking about "the" material in contrast to "the" ideal. Let us realize, instead, that nature is a conflux of materials with which many things can be done, and that ideals are our statements of what we mean to do with them.

Over the centuries, men have pilloried and massacred each other in the name of religion, each convinced of the sanctity of his own purposes, the righteousness of his own cause. But when

we try to find out what the different things men have called religion have in common, we are reduced to the word alone. No,
Dewey concludes, there is not "religion." There are religions.
How can men speaking the tongue of one set of dogmas communicate with those whose language is both different and differently rooted? They cannot. There is no hope, therefore, that
"religion" as we have known it can ever unify mankind, can ever
build that great community that once was only a dream but now
has the power of a working ideal. Let us speak, then, neither of
"religion" nor of "religions." Let us rather face the fact that of
the multitudes of experience possible for human beings, some of
them are religious. An experience is religious when it has a unifying effect. An ideal is religious when it can help to unify experience. We see, consequently, that the ideal of community which is
equivalent to democracy is, in its inclusively unifying quality, a
religious ideal as well.

Try as we will, however, and hope as we must, the upshot
of things does not depend upon us alone. We are part of a larger
whole. We may call this the universe, as long as we are mindful
that it is a universe in the making, as much as our selves are. In
it we are both sheltered and tossed, checked and sustained. We
may upbraid the universe for sometimes frustrating our best ambitions. The real impiety, however, is to ignore the fact that, little
as we are, we would be nothing without it. That we are dependent
upon the wider nature of which we are part has its good as well
as evil side. Sometimes, to be sure, it dashes us to earth. Yet sometimes, too, it lets us climb the peaks from which we get an endless vista of endless possibilities.

# IMPORTANT DATES IN JOHN DEWEY'S LIFE

| | |
|---|---|
| 1859 | Born in Burlington, Vt. |
| 1879 | Graduates from University of Vermont; starts teaching high school in South Oil City, Pa. |
| 1881 | Returns to Burlington, studies philosophic classics and teaches at village school in Charlotte, Vt. |
| 1882 | Decides on career of teaching philosophy, enters Johns Hopkins University |
| 1884 | Receives Ph.D. degree from Johns Hopkins; accepts instructorship in philosophy at University of Michigan |
| 1886 | Marriage to Alice Chipman |
| 1888 | Accepts professorship of philosophy at University of Minnesota |
| 1889 | Returns to University of Michigan as chairman of the department of philosophy |
| 1894 | Goes to the University of Chicago as chairman of the department of philosophy, psychology, and pedagogy |
| 1896 | Founds the Laboratory School |
| 1899 | Becomes president of the American Psychological Association |
| 1904 | Resigns from the University of Chicago faculty, accepts professorship at Columbia University |
| 1905 | Becomes president of the eastern division of the American Philosophical Association |
| 1915 | Helps found and becomes first president of the American Association of University Professors |
| 1916 | Helps found the original teacher union movement in |

|      | New York City, later becoming a charter member of the New York Teachers Guild, American Federation of Teachers |
|------|------|
| 1919 | Visits Japan, lectures at Tokyo Imperial University |
| 1919–21 | Visits extensively in China, lectures at National Universities at Peking and Nanking |
| 1923 | Delivers first series of Carus Lectures before meeting of American Philosophical Association at Columbia University |
| 1927 | Death of Alice Chipman Dewey |
| 1929 | Becomes president of the Peoples Lobby and chairman of the League for Independent Political Action; delivers Gifford Lectures at Edinburgh |
| 1930 | Becomes professor emeritus at Columbia University |
| 1931 | Delivers William James Lectures at Harvard University |
| 1934 | Delivers Terry Lectures at Yale University |
| 1937 | Serves as member of the Commission of Inquiry into the Charges against Leon Trotsky |
| 1946 | Marriage to Roberta L. Grant |

# SELECTED BIBLIOGRAPHY

BOOKS BY JOHN DEWEY

*The School and Society*. Chicago: The University of Chicago Press, 1899; revised edition, 1915.

*Studies in Logical Theory*. Chicago: The University of Chicago Press, 1903.

*Ethics* (with James H. Tufts). New York: Henry Holt and Company, 1908; revised edition, 1932.

*How We Think*. Boston: D. C. Heath & Co., 1910; revised edition, 1933.

*The Influence of Darwin on Philosophy*. New York: Henry Holt and Company, 1910.

*German Philosophy and Politics*. New York: Henry Holt and Company, 1915.

*Schools of Tomorrow* (with Evelyn Dewey). New York: E. P. Dutton & Company, 1915.

*Democracy and Education*. New York: The Macmillan Company, 1916.

*Essays in Experimental Logic*. Chicago: The University of Chicago Press, 1916.

*Reconstruction in Philosophy*. New York: Henry Holt and Company, 1920; enlarged edition, Boston: The Beacon Press, 1948.

*Human Nature and Conduct*. New York: Henry Holt and Company, 1922; Modern Library Edition, 1930.

*Experience and Nature*. Chicago, London: Open Court Publishing Company, 1925; revised edition, New York: W. W. Norton & Co., Inc., 1929.

*The Public and Its Problems.* New York: Henry Holt and Company, 1927.

*Characters and Events* (edited by Joseph Ratner). New York: Henry Holt and Company, 1929, two volumes.

*The Quest for Certainty.* New York: Minton, Balch & Co., 1929.

*Individualism, Old and New.* New York: Minton, Balch & Co., 1930.

*Philosophy and Civilization.* New York: Minton, Balch & Co., 1931.

*Art as Experience.* New York: Minton, Balch & Co., 1934.

*A Common Faith.* New Haven: Yale University Press, 1934.

*Liberalism and Social Action.* New York: G. P. Putnam's Sons, 1935.

*Logic: The Theory of Inquiry.* New York: Henry Holt and Company, 1938.

*Freedom and Culture.* New York: G. P. Putnam's Sons, 1939.

*Problems of Men.* New York: Philosophical Library, 1946.

*Knowing and the Known* (with Arthur F. Bentley). Boston: The Beacon Press, 1949.

## BOOKS ABOUT JOHN DEWEY

Sidney Hook, *John Dewey: An Intellectual Portrait.* New York: The John Day Company, 1939.

Sidney Hook, ed., *John Dewey, Philosopher of Science and Freedom.* New York: The Dial Press, 1950.

Joseph Ratner, introductory essay to volume of Dewey selections edited by him, *Intelligence in the Modern World.* New York: The Modern Library, 1939.

Paul Arthur Schilpp, ed., *The Philosophy of John Dewey.* Evanston and Chicago: Northwestern University, 1939.

*The Philosopher of the Common Man,* Essays in Honor of John Dewey to Celebrate his Eightieth Birthday. New York: G. P. Putnam's Sons, 1940.

# SUPPLEMENT TO BIBLIOGRAPHY

Harold Allen, *Dewey's Criticism of the British Empiricists.* Unpublished M.A. thesis, Columbia University, 1951.

Clifford W. Anderberg, *The Impact of Civilization on Dewey's Theory of Knowledge and the Critics of Dewey.* Unpublished Ph.D. thesis, University of Wisconsin, 1953.

Melvin Charles Baker, *Foundations of John Dewey's Educational Theory.* New York: Columbia University Press, 1955.

Marc Belth, *The Concept of Democracy in Dewey's Theory of Education.* Unpublished Ph.D. thesis, Columbia University, 1956.

John Lawrence Childs, *American Pragmatism and Education: An Interpretation and Criticism.* New York: Holt, Rinehart & Winston, Inc., 1956.

George Raymond Geiger, *John Dewey in Perspective.* New York: Oxford University Press, Inc., 1958.

Corliss Lamont, ed., with the assistance of Mary Redmer, *Dialogue on John Dewey.* Participants: James Thomas Farrell, James Gutmann, Alvin Johnson, Horace Meyer Kallen, Harry Wellington Laidler, Corliss Lamont, Ernest Nagel, John Herman Randall, Jr., Herbert Wallace Schneider, Harold Taylor, Milton Halsey Thomas. New York: Horizon Press, 1959.

Sidney Ratner and Jules Altman, eds., with James E. Wheeler, associate ed., *John Dewey and Arthur F. Bentley: A Philosophical Correspondence, 1932-1951.* New Brunswick, N.J.: Rutgers University Press, 1964.

Edgar Stern Robinson, *John Dewey's Political Thought.* Unpublished Ph.D. thesis, Columbia University, 1953.

# INDEX

Galileo, Galilei, 27
General Welfare, 90 ff.
Genetic Fallacy, 14, 26
Genetic Method, 14 f.
Gengis Khan, 54
George, Henry, 19
Gilman, Daniel Coit, 6

Habit, 20 f., 64 ff., 69 ff., 74 f.
Harris, W. T., 5 ff.
Hegel, G. W. F., 7 f., 10 ff., 17 f., 21, 32
History, 11 ff., 22, 55, 83, 109
Hitler, Adolf, 15, 39, 111
Hodgson, Shadworth, 35
Holmes, Justice Oliver Wendell, 26, 33, 57
Horace, 54
Horney, Karen, 89
Human Nature, 30, Chapter Three, 82, 90, 97 f., 110
Hume, David, 27, 31, 35
Hutchins, Robert M., 74

Ideals, 118 f.
Ideas, 21, 41 ff.
Indeterminate Situation, 42 f., 45
Industrial Democracy, 96, 99 f.
Instincts, 60 ff.
Instrumentalism, 41, 46, 108
Intelligence, 63, 81, 91, 100, 102, 109, 114 ff.

James, William, 8, 10 f., 20 f., 32, 35 ff., 46, 63 ff., 69 f., 75
Jefferson, Thomas, 72
Jesus, 17, 54
Jonson, Ben, 54
Judgment, 116 f.

Kant, Immanuel, 7 f., 26 f., 31
Keats, John, 108
Knowledge, 21, 28, 31, 34, 36 ff., 43, 45 f., 84, 88, 90

Language, 87 ff.
Lenin, Nicolai, 40
Liberalism, 92 ff.
Liszt, Franz, 87
Logic, 44 f.

Madison, James, 101
Marx, Karl, 1, 7, 13 f., 41, 101
Mead, George Herbert, 66
Meaning, 22, 26, 84 ff., 107 f.
Means and Ends, 94
Metaphysics, 29
Michelangelo, 107
Milton, John, 2
Mind, 10 f., 21, 32, 64 f.
Moral Relativism, 109 f.
Morris, George Sylvester, 7
Napoleon, 19, 54
Nature, 18, 28 ff., 40, 47 f., 52, 106
Newton, Isaac, 44

Oedipus Complex, 57
Olivier, Laurence, 104

Peirce, Charles Sanders, 32 ff., 37, 40, 46, 71
Philosophy, 15, 20, 22 ff., 86
Plato, 7, 15 f., 25 f., 62
Pragmatism, 33, 46
Private Enterprise, 90 f., 97 ff.
Progress, 50

Qualities, 27

Radical Empiricism, 32
Realism, 35
Reality, 15 f., 25, 39, 46 f., 51
Relations, 17, 32
Religious Experience, 102, 118 f.
Robinson, Edwin Arlington, 54
Robinson, James Harvey, 19
Royce, Josiah, 33
Russell, Bertrand, 35